the complete guide to

buying, developing & investing in green property

Solar domestic hot water systems are the fastest growing renewable technology in Europe. Germany still leads the way followed by France and although a long way behind, prospects in the UK are much improved and we are now far better placed than ever before to take advantage of the advances in solar domestic hot water technology.

Companies such as Vaillant that that offer all the individual components of the system as well as understanding how they can be combined with existing conventional heating are best placed to maximise the efficiencies of this new technology.

The Vaillant solar domestic hot water system is the most advanced complete solar heating system available and is totally consistent with the company's commitment to providing maximum efficiency, high performance and total reliability.

Vaillant offers two types of solar collector:

- Vaillant's auroTHERM exclusive evacuated tube collectors are manufactured using specially toughened glass for durability and a special high selective absorber coating for efficiency. They are delivered pre-assembled with either 8 or 16 tubes for ease of installation. Panels can be simply pushed together and up to a total of 12 panels can be connected in series to provide an attractive installation. An extensive range of mounting accessories, suitable for pitched or flat roofs and wall fixing, provides total siting flexibility.

- Vaillant's latest edition to the range is the auroTHERM VFK flat plate collector consisting of a toughened 4mm thick solar glass cover with a copper absorber coating. The whole assembly is encased in a polished aluminum frame for a neat construction.

As solar domestic hot water technology does not rely on sunlight but on solar radiation, it can provide around 50-70% of annual domestic hot water requirements – even on a cloudy day!

Using the sun as a renewable energy source helps the environment, leads to reduced energy bills and means less reliance on gas and electricity for water heating.

For more information on Vaillant visit **www.vaillant.co.uk**

WEIGHED, MEASURED, NOT FOUND WANTING

We hear the term sustainable bandied around on a regular basis, and many manufacturers claim that their products are sustainable, often purely on the grounds of some environmentally beneficial quality, without ever truly comprehending what sustainability is all about let alone having a verifiable indicator of it.

One construction manufacturer stands alone in having had the sustainability of its manufacturing processes and products independently and publicly weighed and measured, and in the ensuing results and in its willingness to improve further has not been found wanting.

Market leader Kingspan Insulation first initiated a full sustainability report on the environmental, societal and economic impact of its activities from Arup using its SPeAR tool in 2004. Kingspan is now ready to move into the next phase of its sustainable development programme following the publication of the latest comprehensive report, having undergone a full review in 2005 and a further mid term review in 2006.

Each review has shown clear progress in the four key areas of sustainability: natural resource use and environmental, societal and economic impacts, whilst highlighting where further improvements can be made. The programme of continual assessment informs management decisions about where to invest and develop, and the reports are made publicly available so that stakeholders can clearly see the evidence of sustainable practice.

This last element is crucial and currently unique in the construction industry in being able to assure end users of the sustainable credentials of the products they are specifying and employing.

Arup is revisiting Kingspan Insulation's UK manufacturing site in 2007 to continue the process, in the meantime visit **www.insulation.kingspan.com** to download a copy of the 2006 report or please contact Kingspan Insulation Ltd. on the numbers below:

UK
Tel: **+44 (0) 870 733 8333**
Fax: **+44 (0) 1544 387 299**
Email: **literature.uk@insulation.kingspan.com**

Are you doing your bit?

Look! Not wanting to be over dramatic or anything, but the sands of time are running away. We all have an obligation to act more sustainably. Here is what Kingspan Insulation has been doing.

Back in 2002 Kingspan Insulation was the first insulation manufacturer to openly publish the results of an independently certified Life Cycle Assessment. This BRE Ecoprofile shows the environmental impact that results from the manufacture of Kingspan's high performance rigid urethane insulation products.

But... things have moved on. It is no longer sufficient to while away time talking about the environmental impacts of a product's or company's performance. Impacts on Natural Resources, the Economy and Society should also be considered.

Kingspan Insulation approached renowned consultants ARUP to carry out a holistic Sustainability Appraisal of its largest manufacturing facility at Pembridge, Herefordshire. Kingspan Insulation has again openly published the results of this independent study, again being the first building products manufacturer so to do. More importantly, Kingspan Insulation has published its commitment to implement the raft of improvement actions recommended by the ARUP sustainability team, has completed many already and is working on the balance.

Kingspan Insulation has made a start – HAVE YOU? Perhaps your first decision could be to only use materials from manufacturers that can demonstrate to you what they are doing about the holistic sustainability of their products.

Copies of ARUP's Sustainability Appraisal with Kingspan Insulation's improvement action plan are available from Kingspan Insulation on:

Telephone: 0870 733 8333
email: literature.uk@insulation.kingspan.com

www.insulation.kingspan.com

® Kingspan and the Lion device are Registered Trademarks of the Kingspan Group plc

Kingspan Insulation Ltd
Pembridge, Leominster, Herefordshire HR6 9LA, UK
Tel: 0870 850 8555 Fax: 0870 850 8666
email: info.uk@insulation.kingspan.com

Greenskies solar water heating systems from Worcester.

Have you ever considered the power of the sun to heat your hot water? Have a Worcester Greenskies solar water heating system installed up to around 70%* of your annual hot water requirements could come to you entirely free.

With fuel costs rising dramatically, solar energy makes more sense as every day goes by. It is free, sustainable, renewable energy from one of the most powerful sources of all.

When you choose a Worcester Greenskies solar water heating system you benefit from the reassurance and peace of mind that comes from dealing with an environmentally aware company that is part of the worldwide Bosch Group.

For further details or to find your nearest installer, call 0800 58 14 07 or visit www.worcester-bosch.co.uk

WORCESTER
Bosch Group

Dedicated to heating comfort

*Source: DTI

GRDP

THE LATEST ENERGY EFFICIENT HEATING AND HOT WATER SYSTEMS FROM WORCESTER

As part of their commitment to developing energy efficient heating and hot water systems for the home, Worcester, part of the Bosch Group has a large portfolio of high efficiency oil and gas fired boilers, renewable technologies such as solar water heating systems and ground source heat pumps.

Boilers – all you need to know

One of the biggest causes of high fuel bills and wasted energy comes from older, non condensing boilers usually over 15 years old. Worcester's range of Greenstar condensing boilers carry the Energy Saving Recommended logo, are SEDBUK A rated for efficiency and are over 90% efficient.

An efficient boiler should have a control system which features precise temperature control, automatic temperature modulation and an anti-cycle timer, all of which can help you reduce how much energy you are using. Making small changes such as monitoring how much energy you use, having annual checkups on your heating system and reducing your thermostat setting can make a big difference to your fuel bills and to the environment.

Going solar

Worcester's 'Greenskies' solar water heating system produces up to 70% of a home's hot water requirements, while the condensing boiler produces the rest. This should allow you to turn off your boiler during the summer months. The Greenskies solar panels work even on cloudy days – a blessing, given our notoriously variable weather in the UK.

Neil Schofield, head of sustainable development at Worcester comments, "The rising cost of fuel bills and concerns over climate change have led consumers to consider renewable technologies for heating their homes. More and more homeowners are expressing an interest in, or having our Greenskies solar water heating systems installed."

How do they work?

Very simply, the Greenskies solar water heating panels are slim, double glazed units that usually fit on your roof for maximum sunlight gain. The panels work by absorbing heat and daylight from the sun, which is then transferred through a series of pipes into your hot water cylinder.

The cost

Prices for solar systems have fallen over recent years, and although each installation is unique, you can expect to pay £2,500-£4,000, for the full installation, dependant on the complexities of the installation. There are various grants available and as an added incentive, VAT is payable at 5%. You will need to contact a trained installer and there is a list available sorted by postcodes on the Worcester website: **www.worcester-bosch.co.uk**

Greenstore

Worcester has further expanded its portfolio of energy efficient heating solutions with the launch of 'Greenstore' ground source heat pumps. By taking solar energy from the ground and pumping it into the home, they provide an extremely 'green' alternative to traditional central heating. At their most efficient, this technology is capable of providing up to 75% of your heating and hot water for free.

Neil Schofield comments, "Greenstore really is one of the technologies of the future; it not only reduces household bills but will significantly reduce our impact on the environment. The system is capable of heating the whole home and is particularly suitable for providing under floor heating."

How do they work?

Ground source heat pumps draw energy via collectors laid in the ground which then deliver it to the building. The pump system then compresses the energy, causing the temperature to rise rapidly. This heat is then transferred directly to the heating and hot water system in the house.

Installation Costs

Each installation is unique to the property but typically cost from £8,000-£12,000. The government is offering grants of up to £1,200 under the Low Carbon Building Program to go towards the cost and VAT is payable at 5%.

For more information on Worcester's range of SEDBUK A rated boilers, Greenskies Solar panels and Greenstore ground source heat pumps, visit **www.worcester-bosch.co.uk** or call **08457 256206**.

Floor heating – the green option

Saving the planet and reducing your carbon footprint is one of the hottest topics at the moment, with everybody wanting to make sure they are as eco-friendly as possible. A simple and cost effective answer is to install floor heating in your new property. Technology has advanced considerably in recent years and not only is it now a more affordable means of heating, but also an incredibly energy efficient one, compared with radiator based systems.

New Building Regulations that came into effect in April 2005 will reduce the future environmental impact of buildings, with the aim of a 15% reduction in the amount of energy used by domestic homes. To achieve this, much more emphasise needs to be placed on incorporating low-energy design elements into the initial planning stages.

This need for environmentally friendly heating options has lead to an increase in the sales of floor heating, with options available to suit every type of project – from new build properties and whole house renovations, to single room refurbishments or extensions. Planning a floor heating system into your project allows you or your future buyers to take advantage of a whole range of benefits. As well as being the most comfortable, energy efficient and clean form of heating you can choose, it also frees your walls of unsightly radiators and provides more useable wall space.

Optimum efficiency

Floor heating requires the water to be set at a lower temperature than with radiator based systems, in order to achieve the equivalent heat output. Typically, you can reduce room temperatures by 1-2°C with floor heating, and each 1°C reduction leads to a 6% reduction in fuel consumption.

To achieve optimum efficiency from your floor heating system it should be connected to a condensing boiler. When used in this way, a condensing boiler can work close to its maximum efficiency, whereas with radiators they generally only work at around 88%.

Heating your home through a floor system also lowers the return temperature of the water to the boiler, which reduces carbon emissions further. Whereas, the return temperature in radiator systems is too high for the boiler to work in condensing mode, floor heating produces a much lower return rate, therefore, reducing the carbon emissions produced.

Alternative energy

An ideal way of taking energy efficiency to the next level is to connect your floor heating to an alternative energy source, which will become more commonplace in the future. For example, floor heating will work effectively with a geothermal heat pump, which is 3-4 times more efficient than a condensing boiler. Heat pumps are designed specifically to work economically with lower temperatures, making them ideal for use with floor heating systems, which demand a low temperature rise output from the boiler.

Comfortable environment

The method by which floor heating warms a room also reduces the amount of energy used. They emit gentle radiant warmth across the entire floor surface, ensuring the room is heated evenly, eliminating draughts and cold spots, and ensuring a warm and cosy environment. This produces almost ideal heating conditions, and typically people will feel more comfortable at a lower temperature. Therefore, the room thermostat can be turned down, reducing energy without impacting on comfort levels.

As floor heating reduces air circulation within the room, it minimises airborne dust particles and provides a healthier and allergy free environment for the whole family.

Whatever your project, or choice of heat source, there is a floor heating system for you.

For more information on the benefits of floor heating visit
www.freeyourwalls.com

the complete guide to

buying, developing & investing in green property

catherine dawson

KOGAN
PAGE

Publisher's note
Every possible effort has been made to ensure that the information contained in this book is accurate at the time of going to press, and the publishers and author cannot accept responsibility for any errors or omissions, however caused. No responsibility for loss or damage occasioned to any person acting, or refraining from action, as a result of the material in this publication can be accepted by the editor, the publisher or the author.

First published in Great Britain in 2007 by Kogan Page Limited

120 Pentonville Road
London N1 9JN
United Kingdom
www.kogan-page.co.uk

© Catherine Dawson, 2007

British Library Cataloguing in Publication Data

A CIP record for this book is available from the British Library.

ISBN-10   0 7494 4975 6
ISBN-13   978 0 7494 4975 9

Typeset by JS Typesetting Ltd, Porthcawl, Mid Glamorgan
Printed and bound in Great Britain by Cambrian Printers Ltd, Aberystwyth, Wales

Contents

heuga | country classic

100% wool

Truly unique new carpet tiles especially designed for a soft, natural texture from a 100% pure wool blend.

Sustainable modular flooring, with style

When it comes to choosing flooring for a 'green' property development or investment, many of us would immediately think of materials that are found in nature like stone and wood. However, thinking in that way you could automatically deny yourself choice and eliminate the most comfortable and luxurious type of flooring from your decision process: carpet! It is true that carpet as an end product is not a completely natural product but that does not mean carpet can not be sustainable. With Heuga[1] soft modular flooring there is an alternative! For those of you looking to 'green' your options when choosing materials for your property, without compromising style, Heuga have an answer. This innovative flooring manufacturer has taken the lead in launching the first in a programme of climate neutral carpet tiles for the home. New Country Classic embraces the theme of 'ecology in the home' and is being made in such a way as to support the company's innovative Mission Zero™ environmental commitment; a promise to eliminate completely, any negative impact the company may have on the environment by the year 2020.

Journey to sustainability

Heuga is not just jumping on the bandwagon of sustainability like many other companies do by exploiting going green just from a commercial point of view. These days everyone seems to be claiming to take full responsibility for their impact on the environment by introducing climate neutral products and services. However this usually means nothing more than paying off greenhouse gas emissions without taking further steps to reduce those emissions or investing in developing other green initiatives like waste

[1] Heuga is the European residential division of InterfaceFLOR, a worldwide leader in the manufacture of modular flooring and part of Interface Inc.

reduction or tackling the landfill problem. Unlike these companies Heuga have invested in a long-term, far-reaching journey to sustainability that is not about one product or one process but about the whole system of manufacturing and the entire lifecycle of each product. Heuga began its journey through its parent company, Interface Inc over 13 years ago when founder and Chairman Ray Anderson initiated the mission towards becoming a fully sustainable company by the year 2020. He recognised that business could no longer continue to use up earth's natural resources without regard for the future. Since then Heuga have been working constantly on reducing its negative impact on the planet. This is not an easy task but Heuga are genuinely committed to the Mission Zero goal and have reached some great achievements so far.

Operating from factories which use only green electricity supplies, Interface Inc has reduced the amount of greenhouse gas emissions associated with the manufacture of its products by 60% over the last 13 years; they are now pioneering the use of carbon offsets to balance the remaining emissions created in areas such as transport and employee travel. The offsets work by generating investment in a variety of renewable energy and energy efficiency projects, with the aim of balancing the remaining emissions still generated during manufacture. Additionally Interface Inc has managed to reduce water usage by 81%, energy usage by 41% and landfill waste by 63%. Another example is the company car scheme that is now based on the entire life cycle of the vehicle with choices limited based on longevity and emission levels.

Climate neutral flooring for the home

Creating an environmentally-friendly property has many benefits as well as from an environmental as from an economical point of view. You can help counter climate change and contribute to creating a healthier planet. Moreover using environmentally-friendly materials on the inside, as well as on the outside, of the house increases the value of your property. Heuga's first climate neutral carpet tile Country Classic has everything to meet this twofold benefit. Every square metre comes with a verified, prepaid carbon offset from a leading environmental organisation, Climate Care[2] – a truly unique feature in flooring for the home. Country Classic has a traditional natural Berber look, and has been especially designed for a soft, natural texture from a 100% pure wool blend (63% New Zealand wool for softness, 37% highland wool from Scotland for toughness) the most sustainable of carpet yarns. Additionally Country Classic will also help save on your energy use compared to hard flooring through its superb insulating ability.

The environmental and economical benefits of Country Classic are not compromising its style or quality at all. Country Classic exhibits a timeless look with a feel that is gentle to the touch; all the practicality and quality that is expected from Heuga is still there as well, in a range of brand new colours ranging from creamy Vanilla to rich Macadamia. Like any other Heuga product the design possibilities are endless. Individual designs are simple to create and install, using numerous colour combinations, zones, borders or rug effects; in the event of any serious spills or irreparable damage, the affected area can easily be replaced or repaired.

Country Classic is a truly unique combination of tradition, fashion and environmental care and allows you the freedom to add that touch of personality to your property.

Easy to install – easy to change!

For the 'self-builder', the 50cm modular format of carpet tiles make planning and installing easy – anyone competent with a Stanley knife and

---

[2] Heuga is the European residential division of InterfaceFLOR, a worldwide leader in the manufacture of modular flooring and part of Interface Inc.

straight edge can master that. Furnished spaces do not need to be completely emptied as you can move the items around within the space during the process. No adhesives are needed, just some low-tack tape – wood and other hard surfaces can be easily covered without damage. Compared to conventional carpeting, fitting waste is also dramatically reduced by the 50cm format and, it comes in manageable boxes – much easier for spaces above the ground floor.

When it comes time to change the flooring, they can be removed a section at a time and replaced, then just removed in the boxes from the new tiles – it could not be easier.

End-of-life responsibility

At the moment Heuga are developing another green initiative unique to the flooring industry: a warranty under which Heuga commits to take back the old product at the end of its life and not to landfill it. Collection points where the old product can be returned to are being established across the country. The old tiles will then be re-used, down-cycled or recycled. For example the backing of the tile could be recycled into car mats. With this end-of-life responsibility concept Heuga is taking a pioneer position in the flooring industry. The modular nature of Heuga carpet tiles and the easy, adhesive free installation method are huge benefits compared to broadloom carpet and hard flooring where unwieldy dimensions and toxic finishes are big issues.

Useful links:

www.heuga.com	Heuga website
www.heuga.com/MissionZero/uk	information on Mission Zero™
www.climatecare.org	details on how carbon offsets work
www.interfacesustainability.com	the Interface Inc corporate sustainability site

Introduction

Our planet is experiencing significant climate change. Scientists seem to be in general agreement that it is human activity that is influencing this change, and that if human behaviour is not altered the planet will suffer. Already we are experiencing more extremes of weather – 2006 was the warmest year on record in the United Kingdom, and the 10 warmest years globally since formal records began in 1861 have all occurred since 1994. The temperature in the United Kingdom in 2006 reached 104 ºF (40 ºC), and scientists predict that 2007 will see even hotter temperatures. Water shortages and hosepipe bans are becoming increasingly common in the United Kingdom, while floods and forest fires are causing devastation around the world. If climate change is left unchecked, there will be a profound impact on our way of life and our communities. Agriculture and food production will be seriously affected, water shortages will become more common and population migration will cause serious economic and social problems.

The UK government and environmental groups believe that everyone can and should make a contribution to tackling climate change. In addition to tackling the problems caused by large industry, the government and campaigners believe that individuals can do their part, especially in terms of how they live their lives, the transport they use and the property in which they live.

Everyone has to live somewhere, whether they buy, rent or live in temporary accommodation. In the United Kingdom property has been a good investment for a number of years, with many landlords, investors and developers making considerable profits. Almost every adult in the United Kingdom is involved, in one way or another, with the property market. This book, therefore, is aimed at almost everyone who lives somewhere in the United Kingdom, who is concerned about the environment and who wants to change their behaviour in some way to help our planet.

Chapter 1 addresses the issue of definition – what do we mean by 'green', 'environmentally friendly' and 'global warming'? This chapter goes on to look at personal beliefs and the development of a personal green code that will help us to make important changes. The next 10 chapters of the book are aimed at particular property users – owners, buyers, sellers, landlords, tenants, borrowers, investors, developers, self-builders and gardeners. Many readers will fall into several of these categories, and cross-referencing is provided where appropriate to avoid repetition.

There are many ways to reduce our personal impact on climate change. Some alterations in the way we live and use our property are easy and quick to implement, whereas others may require significant financial outlay and much personal time and dedication to our green project. This book is for people who are interested in making small and/or large changes, and is a practical, down-to-earth, complete guide to green property issues. No prior knowledge is assumed and the book is written in a user-friendly, coherent way, free from technical jargon. Practical information on which you can act is provided, including useful addresses and websites, details of national and local schemes and information about grants, discount schemes and tax incentives.

I hope you enjoy reading this book and find it interesting. I wish you every success with your green project.

1 Making decisions

When we think we are 'green' or 'environmentally friendly', what do we mean? What are the issues and why are they important? What is a 'green' property? What can we do to help the environment as property owners, buyers, sellers, landlords, tenants, investors and developers? What action should we take, and what action do we want and need to take? What personal, environmental and financial benefits can be gained by altering our behaviour?

These are questions that are becoming increasingly important as changes in our climate begin to affect all of our lives. This chapter helps you to think about your environmental philosophy, encouraging you to consider the issues that are important to you, and the aspects of your property decisions that you want to change. Self-evaluation questions are included to help you work through the issues and come to some conclusions. Advice on how to act on these conclusions is offered throughout the rest of the book.

Defining a green property

There are many types of green property, and the type that you choose will depend on a number of factors, including your personal and/or family philosophy, your personal finances, how much time you have available to spend on your green project, your life circumstances and the property in which you currently live.

Green properties can be viewed as being part of a continuum, with households making small but important changes at one end, and newly built eco-houses, using clean, renewable energy sources, at the other end. Where you choose to place yourself on the continuum depends, in part, on the factors listed above. It also depends on your personal motivation to make a conscious choice to improve the place in which you live, or the property that you are intending to buy, sell or use for investment purposes.

All the types of property listed below can be described as 'green' properties, so even if you are constrained by finances or other personal circumstances, there are still some things that you can do to make your property greener. The greenest properties would encompass all the issues listed below:

■ a home or tenanted property in which waste is recycled using local authority recycling schemes and items are reused where possible;

■ a home in which all family members and/or tenants try not to waste energy, by buying energy-efficient appliances and using energy wisely;

■ a tenanted property fitted with energy-efficient appliances in which landlord and tenant adhere to a green code;

■ a home or tenanted property that has switched to green electricity, where a green tariff is paid to use or provide funds for research into renewable energy sources;

■ a renovated property that has been rebuilt and refurbished using green building materials, fixtures and fittings, where possible;

■ a home bought, built or developed with a socially responsible and/or environmentally friendly mortgage;

■ a home in which all property investors and other investors adhere to ethical, social and environmental principles;

■ a newly built property using sustainable and renewable sources of energy and built using green building materials, fitted with the most efficient energy-saving appliances;

■ a zero carbon new home that achieves zero net carbon emissions from energy used in construction and on site over the useful life of the building.

Information about all aspects of these types of green property is presented throughout the rest of this book.

Discovering your environmental philosophy

Why do you want to make your property greener? Some of you may be very worried about the influence of climate change and how this will affect the lives of future generations. Others may be concerned about the unrestricted use of fossil fuels, the prospect of fuel supplies running low and the consequent rise in prices. Or you may be interested in the grants available to help you to become more energy efficient and the prospects of saving money on fuel bills. Or perhaps, as a human being, you are concerned about the welfare of others around the globe. Maybe you want to invest in companies that have the same concerns as you.

Whatever the reasons for wanting to have a greener property, you need to think about these reasons and be honest with yourself. Your reasons will influence the type of property that you buy, the green lifestyle that you choose, the type of development that you undertake and the investment and borrowing opportunities in which you become involved. The following questions will help you to think more about your environmental philosophy:

■ Who, if anyone, has influenced your attitude towards environmental issues?

■ Do you believe that you have received balanced information about the issues involved?

■ Do you know where to obtain impartial and/or balanced information about these issues? (See organizations listed at the end of this book for more information and advice.)

■ What is your attitude towards climate change?

■ Do you understand what causes climate change?

■ Do you believe that you, as an individual, can do anything to reduce climate change?

■ What do you know about energy conservation?

■ Do you believe that you, as an individual, can conserve energy and that it will make a difference if you change your behaviour?

■ What do you know about renewable, sustainable and clean sources of energy?

■ Do you believe, as an individual, that using this type of energy would help the planet?

■ Are you interested in the financial aspect of becoming greener, including government grants and personal savings on energy bills?

■ What are your attitudes towards ethical investment and borrowing?

■ Can you afford to base your investment and property development decisions on ethical principles rather than costs?

You should consider these questions on an individual basis – there are no judgements to be made. If you find that your overriding reason for wanting a greener property is to take advantage of the government grants on offer, then that is fine. This book offers advice for people with all types of green philosophy – taking advantage of grants will still lead to a greener way of life for you and/or your tenants.

Once you have thought about your personal environmental philosophy, you need to think about how this can be matched with your personal circumstances and property aspirations.

Matching your philosophy with personal circumstances

Your personal circumstances will have an influence on the type of green property that you can develop. In particular, if you are a homeowner living with other members of your family, or a property developer or landlord hoping to let your accommodation to tenants, you will need to make sure that others living in your property agree with your environmental philosophy.

You need to work with family members to develop a green code that you all understand and with which you are all happy (see below). This will involve discussing and understanding the pertinent issues. There are a number of books that explain the issues in a way that children can understand, and some of the best books are listed below. Also, schools work hard to teach environmental awareness to children and there are a number of schemes taking place around the country to promote this awareness. More information about these schemes can be obtained from the Energy Saving Trust (EST) website and the National Energy Foundation (NEF) website (details below). Downloadable energy-saving stickers for children are available from the EST website.

Your personal circumstances will have an influence on the amount of time you can devote to your green property. Property owners who work full-time and have other important commitments will not be able to devote as much time to a green property as someone who has decided to leave his or her job to spend the whole time building an eco-home (see Chapter 10). When you think about the type of green property in which you wish to live or invest, you must conduct a realistic evaluation of your present and future time commitments and how much time you are able to spend developing your green property. This is an important consideration for all members of the family – you should not expect others to devote as much time as you if they have little time available or if they are not as strongly motivated.

Matching your philosophy with financial considerations

You will need to consider your personal finances carefully. Some environmental philosophies will help you to save money, for example through energy conservation or through obtaining grants to make home improvements. However, other environmentally friendly changes are expensive, especially in the short term, although you may save money in the long term (see Chapter 2).

It used to be the case that social and environmental investment opportunities were more expensive to set up and provided less potential for growth than less ethically conscious alternatives. However, this is not necessarily the case now. The environmental movement is gaining pace worldwide and more and more environmentally aware companies are being set up, while older companies are changing their traditional practices. When choosing a company in which to invest, or from which to borrow, you need to match your financial circumstances with your environmental philosophy. For example, are you interested in companies that contribute towards a safe and healthy environment, offer ecologically superior products or use ecological principles to drive product design and/or investment (see Chapters 5 and 6)? Would you be willing to pay more for your financial product if it met your ethical/environmental criteria, or would you be willing to compromise on certain principles to obtain a better deal?

It is important to carry out a careful financial assessment when you are formulating your environmental philosophy, so that you are not constrained and disappointed in your plans by lack of finance. Advice is offered throughout this book on the cost of making environmentally friendly changes.

Matching your philosophy with property aspirations

If you are a property developer or an owner intending to sell your property once you have renovated or refurbished, you should note that the EST has found that 64 per cent of potential buyers would not consider houses that have old, damaged boilers, single-glazed windows and insufficient insulation (see Chapters 4 and 9). When developing your property you need to make sure that you have enough finances available to provide the best energy-saving appliances and fixtures that will appeal to your intended market. This could enable you to add considerable sums of money to the potential purchase price, according to the EST and the results of my own research (see Chapter 4). Also, you may be able to take advantage of a government scheme called the Low Carbon Buildings Programme. This is a UK-wide programme that provides grants to individuals, communities and businesses for renewable technologies (see Chapter 9). By developing an environmentally friendly property, you can match you environmental philosophy with your property aspirations and make a good profit at the same time.

From June 2007 anyone intending to sell a property needs to produce a home information pack. Part of this pack involves an energy efficiency assessment. Some people believe that, the higher your property scores in this assessment, the higher price you can charge when selling. Other people are sceptical that this assessment will make any difference – if someone wants a property, he or she will buy it, regardless of the energy efficiency score. However, anyone intending to buy and sell property should consider this issue carefully, balancing energy-efficiency measures with the wants, needs and beliefs of the intended market (see Chapter 4).

As a landlord you will find the letting process easier and more enjoyable if you do not encounter problems with your tenants. One of the ways to do this is to let your property to tenants with whom you have a common bond. Environmental awareness can provide this common bond, and if you advertise your property to like-minded tenants, you should be able to match your personal environmental philosophy with your property aspirations (see Chapter 7).

Developing a green code

You will find it easier to develop and maintain your environmentally friendly property if other household members, tenants and/or business partners are in agreement with you. The easiest way to make sure that you and others know what you are trying to do is to develop a 'green code'. This is a short document that sets out your environmental philosophy in a simple but comprehensive way.

The type of document you produce depends on your green property aspirations. If you are a landlord hoping to let a green property to like-minded tenants, you could produce a green code aimed at your tenants, which describes what you are trying to do and why it is important. The code could be included in your property information pack, and include a set of suggestions about how tenants can help by saving energy, ventilating the property, buying energy-efficient brown goods and reusing and recycling (see Chapter 8).

If you are a householder with partner and children you all need to work together to develop your green code. Children often find this an interesting task, especially when it can be combined with what they are learning at school. If children have been involved with the development of the green code, they are more likely to adhere to the code in the future.

Property developers may find it useful to develop a green code that can be used to help check that builders, suppliers and investors are in agreement with your environmental philosophy. This could include information about sourcing goods, using sustainable and renewable materials, company practices and types of ethical/social investment (see Chapter 9). Companies that consider themselves 'green' will also have a green code that they can supply upon request.

When choosing financial service providers ask to see their code of business ethics, statement of investment principles and/or ethical policy. You can compare these with your own green code to find out whether the company is one in which you wish to invest (see Chapter 6).

Summary

Before you begin to take action to make your property greener, it is useful to think about what you mean by a 'green property'. This will help you to think about the type of action that needs to be taken and why it is important to you, your family, tenants and/or business partner. You can then go on to develop your personal environmental philosophy, which will include all the green issues that are important to you. Once you have done this you can consider your personal circumstances, personal finance, property aspirations and how these match your environmental philosophy.

This chapter has offered advice on these issues and on developing your personal green code. Once you have done this, you can go on to look at specific ways to work within this code. The next chapter offers advice to homeowners who are thinking about making their property greener.

Useful organizations

There are a wide variety of local and national organizations available to offer advice, information, guidance and membership to people who are interested in environmental and property issues.

Energy Saving Trust

The Energy Saving Trust (EST) was established as part of the government's action plan in response to the 1992 Earth Summit in Rio de Janeiro, which addressed worldwide concerns on sustainable development issues. The EST develops and manages programmes on behalf of the UK government, which include awareness-raising among local communities, the general public and commercial organizations; the production and distribution of a wide range of information documents and publications; and grants for innovative technologies and techniques.

Energy Saving Trust (England)
21 Dartmouth Street
London SW1H 9BP
Tel: 020 7222 0101
Fax: 020 7654 2460
www.est.org.uk

Energy Saving Trust (Scotland)
112/2 Commercial Street
Leith
Edinburgh EH6 6NF

Tel: 0131 555 7900
Fax: 0131 555 7919

Energy Saving Trust (Wales)
Wales Albion House
Oxford Street
Nantgarw
Cardiff CF15 7TR
Tel: 01443 845030
Fax: 01433 845940

Energy Saving Trust (Northern Ireland)
Enterprise House
55/59 Adelaide Street
Belfast BT2 8FE
Tel: 028 9072 6006
Fax: 028 9023 9907

Community Action for Energy

This organization is a network of people who share a common interest in community energy projects and ideas. It is a programme from the EST that is designed to 'promote and facilitate local community-based energy projects'. Membership is free and once you become a member you can receive information about training sessions, new initiatives, local funding opportunities and relevant local news.

On its website you can access a database of funding opportunities. This enables you to search by keyword, fund name, type of funding, eligible regions and funding organizations. This is a useful database for finding information about grants and schemes that may benefit you as a homeowner, landlord, developer or tenant. More information about the Community Action for Energy network can be obtained from www.est.org.uk/cafe or by telephoning 08701 261 444.

National Energy Foundation

The National Energy Foundation (NEF) is an educational charity registered in England that helps people in the United Kingdom by offering advice about safe and efficient energy use. On its website you can find information about carbon dioxide emissions, energy ratings, saving energy, renewable and sustainable energy, and subscribe to its free newsletter.

The National Energy Foundation
Davy Avenue
Knowlhill
Milton Keynes MK5 8NG
Tel: 01908 665555
Fax: 01908 665577
E-mail: info@nef.org.uk
Website: www.nef.org.uk

The Carbon Trust

The Carbon Trust is an independent company funded by the government. The role of the company is to help the United Kingdom 'move to a low carbon economy by helping business and the public sector reduce carbon emission now and capture the commercial opportunities of low carbon technologies'. The company produces useful information on climate change and energy efficiency for businesses, provides energy efficiency loans of £5,000–200,000 and advises on Enhanced Capital Allowances for business, including landlords and property developers (see Chapters 7 and 9).

The Carbon Trust
8th floor, 3 Clement's Inn
London WC2A 2AZ
Tel: 0800 085 2005
Fax: 020 7170 7020
E-mail: customercentre@carbontrust.co.uk
Website: www.carbontrust.co.uk

The Carbon Trust in Wales
Albion House, Oxford Street
Nantgarw
Cardiff CF15 7TR
Tel: 01443 845944
E-mail: contactwales@thecarbontrust.co.uk

The Carbon Trust in Scotland
Brunel Building, James Watt Avenue
Scottish Enterprise Technology Park
East Kilbride G75 0QD
Tel: 01355 581810
E-mail: john.stocks@thecarbontrust.co.uk

The Carbon Trust in Northern Ireland
Unit 9, Northern Ireland Science Park
The Innovation Centre
Queen's Road, Queen's Island
Belfast BT3 9DT
Tel: 02890 737912
E-mail: geoff.smyth@thecarbontrust.co.uk

Sustainable Energy Policy Division

For more information about government policy issues relating to
energy efficiency, consult the Sustainable Energy Policy Division of
DEFRA:

Sustainable Energy Policy Division, DEFRA
6/H15 Ashdown House, 123 Victoria Street
London SW1E 6DE
Tel: 020 7082 8709
Fax: 020 7082 8708

Home improvement agencies

Home improvement agencies (HIAs) are small, non-profit-making
bodies that are funded by local authorities through the Supporting
People Programme. They are managed locally by housing associations, local authorities or charitable organizations. The main functions of HIAs are to support vulnerable people in their quest to
remain independent in their homes, help people access funds and
resources to make home improvements, including energy efficiency
improvements, and provide information on home insurance, loans
and equity release. If you are a vulnerable homeowner or a landlord
letting your property to tenants who are older, disabled or on low
incomes, you can seek advice from your local HIA.

More information about HIAs can be obtained from your local authority or by contacting Foundations, which is the national coordinating body for home improvement agencies in England. On its website you can find contact details of your nearest HIA.

Foundations
Bleaklow House, Howard Town Mill
Glossop
Derbyshire SK13 8HT
Tel: 01457 891 909
Fax: 01457 869 361
E-mail: foundations@cel.co.uk
Website: www.cel.co.uk/foundations

Useful websites

www.climnet.org
The Climate Action Network (CAN) is a worldwide network of over 365 non-governmental organizations working to promote action on limiting the human influence on climate change. On its website you can find information about climate change trends and signals, along with information about CAN offices.

www.climate-concern.com
Climate Concern UK is a campaign group focused on increasing public understanding of the dangers of climate change. On the website you can obtain information about the effects of climate change and useful arguments that help to combat scepticism over climate change.

Further reading

Useful green books for individuals and families include the following:

Callard, S and Millia, D (2001) *The Complete Book of Green Living*, Carlton Books, London
Corkhill, M (2006) *Green Parenting*, Impact Publishing, Bath
Hegarty, M (2000) *The Little Book of Living Green*, Nightingale Press, Royston

Jones, E (2006) *Go Make a Difference*, 3rd edn, Think Books, London

Norris, S (2005) *Superkids! 250 incredible ways for kids to save the planet*, Think Books, London

Siegle, L (2001) *Green Living in the Urban Jungle*, Green Books, Totnes

Trask, C (2006) *It's Easy Being Green: A handbook for earth friendly living*, Gibbs Smith, Layton, Utah

2 Homeowners

As a homeowner there are many things that you can do to make your property greener. Now that you have thought about your green philosophy and defined the environmental issues that are important to you and your family, you can go on to think about the changes that you can make around your home.

This chapter offers practical advice about what you can do to make your home more energy efficient, including information about buying energy-efficient products; advice on converting to renewable energy sources, including costs associated with conversion and the savings that can be made; information about reusing and recycling, and advice about grants and discount schemes for homeowners in the United Kingdom.

Becoming more energy efficient

There are both small and large changes that you, as a homeowner, can make to become more energy efficient. Some of these changes are easy to implement and cost very little, whereas others require the installation of new equipment that may be expensive in the short term, but that will save money and energy in the long term.

Heating and hot water

The EST points out that old boilers account for around 60 per cent of all domestic carbon dioxide emissions. However, if you use a high-efficiency condensing boiler this figure is significantly reduced and you may save in the range of £190–240 a year on your heating bills. Installing a new boiler can be expensive, and, depending on the system and plumber you choose, could be in the region of £800–3,000. However, if the EST savings assumptions are correct, and since most

EVERYTHING YOU NEED FOR
A SOLAR THERMAL SYSTEM*

Solarflo from Baxi

Solarflo – Baxi's solar thermal domestic hot water system

Why utilise solar energy?

Solar energy is a free, renewable power source which, when harnessed, can be converted into heat to generate hot water for the home. Fossil fuels are not infinite, and prices continue to rise. By exploiting the sun's energy, domestic carbon dioxide emissions can be reduced and fuel bills cut.

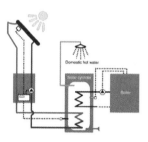

In summer, 100 per cent of the domestic hot water demand can be satisfied using solar collector panels. Even on the greyest winter's day 100 W/m^2 can be produced, and the annual average across the UK is 50-60 per cent.

To make it easier for householders to play their part in tackling climate change, Ruth Kelly, Secretary of State for Communities and Local Government, recently announced the launch of a consultation recommending that people will no longer need to apply for planning permission to install 'microgeneration' devices on their properties.

This means it will be easier than ever to install solar thermal domestic hot water systems.

Solar water heating and the home

Solar water heating is the most popular of the renewable technologies that are presently available, because it is affordable, cost effective and uses proven technology.

For best results the property should have a south facing roof, and not be obstructed by shadows from chimneys or trees. However, it is still possible to carry out an east-west installation by putting a collector panel on each side of the roof to capture maximum energy throughout the day.

Panels can be either on-roof, most common when retro-fitted on existing properties, or in-roof, where the panels are built into the structure of the roof and lie flush with the tiles, generally used for newbuild installations.

Baxi Solarflo can be installed in as little as two days. An initial survey of the site is carried out to ensure the property's suitability and to determine the capacity of the solar cylinder and number of solar collectors, based on the size of the property and hot water requirements.

At least 30 per cent of the cylinder's capacity must be dedicated to solar only, and this must be taken into consideration when calculating hot water requirements during winter months when there is little or no solar gain.

The system has a low environmental impact and can reduce the carbon dioxide emissions of the property by up to a tonne per year. As more people make changes to their lifestyle, and adopt new technologies, such as solar thermal hot water systems, the UK's carbon emissions will continue to fall, as will homeowner's energy costs.

How Baxi Solarflo works

Roof mounted solar collector panels absorb and convert free energy from the sun's rays, which heats a mixture of water and glycol. This liquid, entirely sealed within the system, is circulated through a solar coil in the base of a specially designed Megatech Solar cylinder. This heats the stored water, which is then available for use at the hot taps.

If necessary, additional hot water can be produced using the conventional boiler and the second coil in the cylinder, or electric immersion heater, depending on the sort of Megatech cylinder installed and fuel type.

The Baxi Solarflo solar thermal domestic hot water system is a complete package including solar collector panels, a twin coil solar cylinder and the heat transfer system, along with all the ancillary accessories needed to complete the installation.

Baxi offers fully accredited solar installation training and national technical support and after-sales service. The solar cylinder has a 25 year warranty, and the Solarflo collector panels have a 10 year warranty. For more information call Baxi on **08706 060623**.

boilers have an expected lifetime of 10–15 years, you should recoup the costs and make considerable savings by replacing your old boiler. Although these figures appear convincing, it is important to note that there are wide variations in the costs and savings that can be made, and that these will be influenced by property size and type, local climate, type of heating controls, your existing boiler, occupancy patterns and existing insulation. Therefore, it is important to seek appropriate advice before making changes to your present system.

For independent, professional advice about heating and hot water systems and to find a qualified installer consult the Heating and Hot Water Industry Council website (www.centralheating.co.uk). You can find out more about the energy efficiency of boilers by using the database at www.boilers.org.uk before you make your purchase. This website provides useful information about the costs and savings that can be made by changing your existing boiler. If you are on certain benefits, grants may be available through Warm Front, Warm Homes, Warm Deal and the Home Energy Efficiency Scheme (see below). Some local authorities provide grants for the installation of heating systems (see Appendix 1).

Loft insulation

Up to a third of all heat lost in a home can be through poor insulation in roof spaces, according to the EST. However, loft insulation is quick and easy to install and there are green products available, including insulation made from fire-retarded recycled newspaper and from British sheep's wool. These products are safe to install, easy to cut with a sharp knife or shears and do not need any special protective clothing, apart from a simple dust mask. It costs around £150–400 to install loft insulation, depending on the product you choose and the size of your loft, and you could save £60–70 per year on heating bills, according to the NEF. Grants and discounts are available for loft insulation (see Appendix 1).

If you choose to install loft installation yourself, useful information about where and how to install environmentally friendly products can be obtained from the Green Building Store website (www. greenbuildingstore.co.uk). For more information about installing loft insulation effectively and safely contact the NEF (see Chapter 1). If you choose to use an installer, contact the National Association of Loft Insulation Contractors for information about contractors in your area (details below).

Wall insulation

There are three types of wall insulation, and the type that you install depends on the property in which you live. Cavity wall insulation is the most common, and involves the injection of blown mineral wool, urea formaldehyde foam or polystyrene beads into the wall cavities. Although these cannot be considered 'green' insulation materials, you will save energy by having them installed: you could save up to £70 a year, according to the NEF. Installation costs vary, depending on the size of your house, the contactor you use and the type of insulation material, but should be in the region of £200–500 if you take advantage of local discount schemes. All insulation materials must meet government standards, and you should use an approved contractor to carry out the work, as the installation then will be guaranteed for 25 years by the Cavity Insulation Guarantee Agency (details below).

The other two types are internal and external wall insulation. These involve the installation of flexible thermal lining, rigid thermal board or external cladding/render. Costs can range from £500–5,000, depending on the size of your house, the contractor you use and the type of insulation required. An approved installer in your area for all types of insulation can by found by consulting the National Insulation Association (NIA) website (details below). Grants and discounts are available for certain types of wall insulation (see the Appendix).

Floor insulation

The EST estimates that you could save up to £50 a year by installing floor insulation, although again, these savings depend on a number of factors such as size of property, type of flooring, other insulation and type of heating. Depending on your current flooring and the amount of work you wish to undertake, there are various options available to you. Perhaps one of the quickest and simplest ways to reduce draughts through floorboards is to fill gaps with a tube sealant. Other popular methods for timber floors include the installation of insulation boards, although there are now more environmentally friendly materials available such as wool quilts and plant-fibre board. All timber flooring insulation should leave a ventilation gap and should not block air bricks, to prevent rotting.

For solid floors, options include polystyrene or foamed glass below floor slabs, or polystyrene or mineral wool above floor slabs, laid

Safe as....

Choosing a new conservatory or replacement windows but don't know who to trust?

Every GGF member must work within our Code of Good Practice. Every one that installs conservatories, windows and doors is also registered with FENSA to simplify working within the new Building Regulations. We offer a scheme to secure your deposit and even an arbitration and conciliation service if a problem can't be solved by other means.

So why not visit our home – www ggf.org.uk – to find out why looking for the GGF logo helps you to rest easy in your home.

It can even help you to choose your installer with complete lists of members of our two specialist groups, the Conservatory Association and the Window and Door Group.

Glass and Glazing Federation

Give your home kerbside appeal

Windows and Doors – what you need to know

Windows are the first thing people see when they visit your house, so it's no surprise to learn that badly fitted windows can affect the value of your home. Your best bet is to choose a member of the Glass and Glazing Federation (GGF).

Especially as all replacement glazing now comes under Building Regulations Control.

This means that if you want to replace your windows, those new windows will have to be energy efficient. The reason for this is the Government's drive to ensure we, like the rest of the world, pollute the atmosphere as little as possible.

If in the future you then decide to sell your property, the purchaser's solicitors, when undertaking the necessary search, will ask for evidence that any replacement windows installed after April 2002 comply with the new Regulations.

You can prove that your windows comply in two ways:-

1. a certificate showing that the work has been done by an installer who is registered under the FENSA Registration Scheme.

   or

2. a certificate from the local authority saying that the installation has approval under the Building Regulations.

If you want to ensure that you comply with these Regulations and that the company undertaking the work will do a good job, you should make sure that you use a Glass and Glazing Federation (GGF) member who is FENSA Registered.

How do I save energy by fitting Energy Rated Windows?

The BFRC Domestic Window Energy Rating Scheme produces a single number to rank a specific window type. A higher BFRC Rating number indicates a more thermally efficient window. The scheme can be applied to all domestic type windows which are installed in the UK.

Correctly designed and installed windows will significantly reduce energy usage. Modern energy efficient windows offer extraordinary thermal performance. Standard double glazing is not the same thing as high performance windows! Energy efficient windows are not dependent on the framing material used. It is possible to make a thermally efficient window from almost any conventional frame material. Some materials are less thermally efficient than others but good design and manufacture can produce high performance windows from any of the common framing materials. Window energy rating clearly identifies the best performing window as a whole system rather than simply concentrating on the frame or glass. If new or replacement windows are being fitted then the extra cost to specify and fit high performance windows is small and the savings and benefits are significant in both the short and the long term. Window energy rating acts as a driving force for improved window energy efficiency by clearly stating the relative efficiency of each type of window. Users and specifiers can select the most suitable window on the basis of cost and benefits.

When you choose a GGF Member, you can be assured that they:

1. Will comply with the new Building Regulations (relating to windows) and ensure you get the appropriate certificate via the Fenestration Self Assessment Scheme (FENSA).

2. Will have been in business for at least three years.

3. Have all been vetted to ensure they provide a quality service, the vetting procedure includes taking up references, looking at their accounts and site visits.

4. Work to the Federation's Code of Good Practice and technical guidelines.

In addition the GGF will provide you with:

1. A free conciliation service – should you and a Member company not see eye to eye over work carried out.

2. Protection for your deposit – the GGF Deposit Indemnity Scheme is backed by Norwich Union and safeguards deposits up to £3,000 or 25% of the contract price, whichever is lower.

3. A Customer Charter.

TRUST MARK
Registered through:
Glass and Glazing
Federation

Contact us on: **0870 042 4255** for a list of members in your area or see **www.ggf.org.uk**

in conjunction with new flooring. Rubber-based materials and cork may offer more environmentally sound alternatives, when obtained from sustainable sources. Prices vary enormously, depending on the type of insulation you choose. Contact the NIA for more information (details below).

Draught-proofing

Draught-proofing measures will help to save energy in your home but you must also make sure that there is adequate ventilation to reduce the build-up of condensation and damp, especially in the bathroom and kitchen, and provide adequate air flow for fires to burn safely. Simple draught-proofing that can be carried out quickly and easily includes the use of brushes, strips, foams, sealants, weather bars or draught excluders on internal and external doors, windows, letterboxes, keyholes and cat flaps.

The installation of double or triple-glazed windows is a popular, but controversial, energy-saving measure. The EST argues that new double or triple-glazed windows help to save energy and can help to add value to your house. However, environmentalists argue that this is leading to a culture of unnecessary window replacement, and that it is more environmentally friendly to cut down on waste and keep and maintain existing windows. Although they may be old they will last many years with careful maintenance, and you can consider installing secondary double glazing to reduce draughts.

Environmentalists argue that the use of PVC window frames should be phased out, as much more energy is used to manufacture PVC than conventional wooden window frames, the plastic is very hard to recycle, it is made from oil and these resources are running out, and the processing during manufacture gives off chemicals that are damaging to the environment. Also, some environmentalists believe that PVC window frames may need replacing more often and are not as durable as manufacturers would lead us to believe. Window frames made from wood that comes from carefully managed forests are a more environmentally friendly option than PVC, but they tend to be more expensive to buy. You need to think about your environmental philosophy, consider the existing windows of your property and decide upon the best option for your personal circumstances and finances. For an interesting comparison of timber versus plastic frames consult www.ambassadoor.co.uk.

If you decide to install double or triple glazing, the air gap between the panes should be 12–20 millimetres and you should specify 'low-e'

Light bulb technology has changed dramatically since Swan in Britain and Edison in the USA, received patents for the traditional incandescent bulb in the late 1870s. Now energy efficient lighting has become a viable, cost effective and environmentally friendly method of lighting homes, offices hotels and commercial establishments without the need for special wiring or installation.

Home energy use accounts for 27 percent of UK CO_2 emissions. Switching to energy efficient lighting will help protect the environment. It also makes financial sense with the rising cost of electricity and the tightening of the UK building regulations.

A standard incandescent bulb typically produces 15 lumens per watt, lumen being a measure of light output, and lasts approximately 1000 hours. A CFL (Compact Fluorescent Lamp), such as the Spyra-lite sold by Initial Lights, produces between 50 and 100 lumens per watt and lasts over 30,000 hours making it far more efficient and cost effective. LEDs (Light Emitting Diodes) surpass this, producing 120 lumens per watt and lasting on average 40,000 hours. Both CFLs and LEDs have their place when considering energy efficient and environmentally friendly lighting. CFLs emit a good range of non directional light whereas LEDs are robust making them ideal for locations where they may be knocked or suffer from vibration.

Low Energy lighting is set to change the way we light our communities. The benefits of energy saving lighting (durability, long life span, low power consumption, low heat) cannot be ignored in today's world where there is an increasing need to conserve resources and reduce energy consumption.

Initial Lights are specialists in the supply of energy saving lighting which is CE approved and RoHS compliant. They know that energy saving lighting will become the industry standard for many lighting applications in the future. That is why they have invested heavily in promoting the technological improvements needed. They are one of the first UK companies to specify innovative designs so that energy saving lighting can be used in a wide spectrum of applications.

For more information and a catalogue please visit their website **www.initiallights.co.uk** or phone **+44(0) 845 094 6054** or e-mail us at: **info@initiallights.co.uk**

Energy Efficient Lighting
Initial Lights

Initial Lights **are based in Macclesfield, Cheshire. We supply a large range of energy efficient products designed to meet current building regulations, reduce CO_2 emissions and save you money. All our products are competitively priced, and have been tested by the UK lighting association for conformance and safety.**

The Brilliance series of lamps are designed to give off low heat with no UV or IR light radiation. Stylish design and environmentally friendly, these lights do not contain any hazardous materials (ROHS compliant). LEDs have a lifetime of upto 50,000 hours which is many times longer than other forms of energy efficient lighting. Brilliance lamps work with worldwide electrical systems (GU10 100~240V AC/MR16 12V DC). They achieve directional light output equal to 25W halogen lamps yet consume 80% less power. Brilliance lamps are ideal for architectural lighting, spot lighting, display cases, mood lighting and many more applications.

CUT YOUR LIGHTING BILL BY 80%
SPYRA~LITE™

Spyra-lite™ is a revolutionary new form of low energy lighting. Using new 'cold-cathode' technology they create light not heat, and are compatible with UK standard MR11, MR16 & GU10 fittings*.

- **Power Consumption only 4w – typically 1/5th of most halogens**
- **Light output of a 20W conventional spotlight**
- **Long lasting – Up to 30 times longer than an incandescent bulb!**
- **Environmentally friendly – contains no hazardous chemicals or substances**
- **CE Marked – Complies with UK & European regulations**

(* Spyra-Lite power supply required)

ALL products carry a full 12 month guarantee
Contact us for further information:

Tel: +44 (0) 845 094 6054
e-mail: info@initiallights.co.uk
web: initiallights.co.uk

Tested and approved by the
UK Lighting Association
Spyra-Lite has been tested in
accordance with BSEN60598-1:
2004 Clauses 13.2.1, 13.3.1 and 13.3.2

Make the Switch™

www.initiallights.co.uk

glazing, which has a special heat-reflective coating between the panes. It is also possible to have argon-gas-filled windows that transmit heat less readily and help to save more money. The British Fenestration Rating Council (BFRC) provides information about choosing the most energy-efficient doors and windows (details below). Prices for double and triple glazing vary enormously, but you should be able to recoup some of the costs from savings on your heating bill over the long term. Grants for draught-proofing measures are available for homeowners and tenants on certain benefits (see below).

Lighting

Although energy-efficient lighting is initially more expensive to install then conventional lighting, considerable savings can be made over its lifetime. Compact fluorescent lamps (CFLs) are modern energy-saving light bulbs, sold by wattage, which fit into standard light fittings. Because they use less electricity you can have a lower wattage bulb to give the same amount of light. When buying light bulbs, look for the new European Energy Label to check that the bulb has an A rating for energy efficiency (see below). Recommended retailers can be obtained from the EST website (see Chapter 1).

Electricity

Simple changes around the home can save electricity and money. These include:

■ switching lights off when out of rooms;

■ not leaving appliances on stand-by or charging unnecessarily;

■ using the economy and half wash buttons on washing machines and tumble driers;

■ not filling the kettle too much when boiling water;

■ utilizing 'one-pot' cooking strategies and cooking more than one dish in the oven at a time;

■ defrosting naturally, rather than using the microwave;

■ using off-peak (night-time) electricity as this is cheaper;

■ using rechargeable batteries where possible and practical;

▊ turning off computer peripherals when not in use and utilizing power-saving options.

Although the energy savings from each of these individual activities are very small, your energy and financial savings will grow in the long term through reducing wastage and changing the habits of every household member.

Smart meters

Smart metres are a new generation of devices that can be installed in houses, replacing existing gas and electricity meters. Using a smart meter, homeowners can monitor their energy output in monetary terms rather than kilowatt hours and find out which equipment is using more energy. If the meters are strategically placed, this monitoring is an easy process, and organizations such as Energywatch believe that this will lead to less energy consumption and make households more responsible in their usage. Smart meters can be read remotely with information sent automatically to the supplier, thus doing away with the need for estimated bills and associated paper wastage.

At this present time smart meters are being piloted in London to find out whether people do change their habits as a result of the meter and to determine which system works best. More information about smart meters can be obtained from the Office of Gas and Electricity Markets website (www.ofgem.gov.uk).

Carbon offset schemes

Today there are a variety of schemes being set up that enable you to offset your known carbon emissions by paying towards replenishing carbon stocks. Through these schemes you can work out how much carbon you use through travel and in your home, and decide how you wish to compensate for this usage. For example, you could invest in schemes that help to increase soil fertility and rehabilitate degraded land in countries that suffer from severe drought, or invest in reforestation schemes.

However, at this present time, this is a youthful, unregulated market and there has been controversy about the benefits of some carbon offset schemes and some fraudulent companies operating.

Other companies are making huge profits, which concerns environmental campaigners. If you choose to follow this route you need to conduct careful research into the scheme and company that you choose. The Climate Group is currently working on an international set of voluntary standards for companies offering carbon offset schemes, and more information and advice can be obtained from this organization (details below).

Buying energy-efficient products

When buying energy-efficient products, there are two logos that you should look for. The first is the EU energy label, which rates products from the most to least efficient. By law this label must be displayed on all refrigeration and laundry appliances, dishwashers, electric ovens and light bulb packages. The second is the energy saving recommended logo which can be found on the following products:

- light bulbs and light fittings;
- fridges and freezers;
- washing machines and dryers;
- dishwashers;
- gas boilers and oil boilers;
- hot water cylinders;
- heating controls;
- loft insulation;
- cavity wall and solid wall insulation;
- glazing;
- integrated digital televisions.

Products that carry this logo have met strict energy-efficient criteria that have been set by the EST. You can find energy-saving recommended products and retailers by visiting the EST website (see Chapter 1).

Plug into nature

100% renewable electricity

Good Energy supplies electricity which has been generated from wind, solar and small-scale hydro to homes and business across the UK via the national grid. **Take a small step, make a big difference** – change today.

For each unit of electricity our customers use we buy one from a renewable source and supply it to the national grid.

Good Energy

Good Energy is the 100% renewable electricity supplier in the UK. We want to let people become part of the solution to Climate Change. By choosing 100% renewable electricity, individuals are cutting their carbon emissions and helping to build a secure energy future.

Today, we supply over 20,000 homes and businesses across the UK with 100% renewable electricity. The energy we supply comes from over 300 independent, renewable generators. They use wind, small-scale hydro and solar power to generate electricity.

We are not a big or faceless company only in the market to sell power. We believe in small-scale, renewable generation and locating these generators close to where the power they make is used provides the best solutions to our environmental and energy needs. This is why we have pioneered schemes which support these generators, making it easy for them to get the payment they deserve.

Educating and empowering individuals is really important to us and we think supporting the market in this way helps to grow renewables. Through Good Energy's events, forums, newsletters, and our educational website, we get people involved with renewables and inspire many to become generators and customers. We are a young team that is committed to making a difference and from our office in rural Wiltshire, we take our mission to the whole of the UK.

How Good Energy works – When you buy electricity you are paying your supplier to put power into the national grid which is linked directly to your home. The grid is like a big water reservoir – lots of suppliers fill it and we all drink from it. The question is how do you want the electricity you are paying for to be made – from coal, nuclear and gas or from green sources?

By choosing 100% renewable electricity, each Good Energy customer cuts their home's carbon footprint by one third, on average. Since Good Energy began, the renewable electricity that our customers have paid for has prevented 107,000 tonnes of carbon dioxide, the principle global warming gas, from being released into our atmosphere. That is equal to the amount of carbon dioxide that would be produced by driving 200 million miles in a petrol engine car – that would get you to the sun and back!

The Good Energy team at their office in Rural Wiltshire

The more customers we have, the greater the demand for renewable energy. Good Energy and our customers are helping to make renewable power an integral piece of the UK's energy mix.

"For those consumers who want a green electricity supply, pure and simple, this is probably the closest they will get to it."
Virginia Graham, National Consumer Council

Supporting the UK's Microgenerators

At **Good Energy**, we support individuals, communities and businesses that generate their own electricity by paying them for their power. The government states that 40% of the UK's electricity could come from microgeneration by 2050. We want to help make this a reality.

Good Energy Home Generation pays people who generate electricity at home for every unit they produce, including the ones they use on site. Good Energy takes care of the paperwork so getting paid for the electricity is made simple. All anyone needs to do is to sign up to Good Energy's 100% renewable electricity supply and install a generator.

In May 2006 Tim and Fiona Start installed a 3kW solar array at their home in Herefordshire. Tim and Fiona love the rural setting in which they live and care for their environment. It's difficult to have a small carbon footprint when you live in a Victorian house in a rural area, but they take simple, effective measures like walking, cycling and using public transport (but not flying). They grow their own vegetables and buy local produce, preferring to shop locally and creatively (and secondhand where possible). They practice recycling and composting and opt against an

Tim and Fiona Start's Home in Hereford that generates electricity using solar power

overly warm centrally heated house – they heat their home with woodburners running on offcuts. Since installing their solar panels The Starts have really begun to make big cuts to their carbon emissions.

"The roof on our house faces south. So we knew that solar panels would make the most of the sun's energy. Our 3kW array produces about three quarters of the electricity we have needed until now. The remainder is supplied by Good Energy which sources all its power from renewable generation. We hope also to install solar thermal panels, which will save a lot of electricity by significantly reducing the need for an immersion heater. A wind turbine might be on the cards as well, eventually.

We believe that climate change is a threat to us all but we realise that there are so many things we can do to become part of the solution. Generating our electricity from solar power is just one way that we can really make a difference." Tim and Fiona Start.

Good Energy's seven steps to becoming a Home Generator

1. Evaluate Have you got sun, the wind or do you have a stream? Choose to tap the energy from the best resource you have.

2. Make your choice Once you know your resource, find the right size of generator to meet your needs. Visit **www.regensw.co.uk** or **www.nef.org.uk** for advice on choosing the right resource and generator for you.

3. Find your installer You know what you need, now find a company who can make it happen. The organisations above can point you to accredited installers.

4. Do your sums Calculate your generator and installation costs and determine how much you will save on your electricity bills and earn from selling your electricity over the life of your generator. You need to consider: the amount of energy you use, the total amount you will generate and the amount of energy you can expect to sell. Your installer can tell you your generation expectation and Good Energy can tell you the value of your electricity.

5. Get a grant When you have the costs for your project you can apply for a Low Carbon Buildings grant. Visit **www.lowcarbonbuildings.org.uk** for information on grants for projects big or small. NB – to better your chances of receiving a grant, make your home as energy efficient as possible.

6. Decision time Once you know if your grant application is successful, it is time to decide if you are going to complete your project. Get out the cheque book and make that call.

7. Get paid Whatever the amount of renewable electricity you are generating, it has a value. To get paid for what you generate, visit **www.good-energy.co.uk**

Good Energy's recent achievements

Winner of a 2006 Green Award

Finalist for the 2006 Green Award Grand Prix

Winner of Woman in Ethical Business Award 2006

Winner of a 2006 Ashden Award for Sustainable Energy

Finalist RegenSW Green Energy awards 2005

Good Energy was the only company awarded Top Marks in The Ethical Company Organisation 2006 research

To find out more about Good Energy call **0845 456 1640**
or visit **www.good-energy.co.uk**

Converting to renewable energy sources

In the United Kingdom, most of the energy that we use is generated through burning coal, gas and oil and by nuclear power stations. Burning fossil fuels releases millions of tonnes of carbon dioxide into the atmosphere each year, and nuclear power production produces harmful waste that can have a devastating impact on the environment. Using energy produced from renewable sources helps to combat these problems, yet only a fraction of energy production in the United Kingdom at present, comes from these sources. It is possible for individual homeowners to increase the use of renewable energy, either by generating their own electricity, or by signing up to a green tariff or green fund.

If you are thinking about converting to a renewable energy source, look for companies that are members of the Renewable Energy Assurance Scheme and products that carry the Renewable Energy Association Listed mark. These ensure that companies and products have met required standards in terms of services and quality. More information about these schemes can be obtained from the Renewable Energy Association (details below).

Generating electricity in the home from renewable sources

There are several types of renewable sources of energy available. Some of these will be more suitable and viable than others, and the choice depends on where you live, the natural resources available and your personal finances. Some renewable sources attract grants and tax incentives, as detailed below.

Hydro power

Hydro power harnesses the energy of moving or falling water. As a homeowner you may find it possible to develop a mini-hydro system to power your own home, or produce a larger hydro system to produce extra kilowatts to sell to the national grid. Costs depend on the system you choose and the amount of groundwork required, and may range from £4,000–25,000. Tax incentives are available in the form of a reduced VAT rate of 5 per cent on hydro-electric plant for systems supplying residential buildings. Also, through the government's Low Carbon Buildings Programme (LCBP), a maximum of a £5,000 grant is offered to individuals and communities that choose equipment from an approved list and use a registered installer (see Appendix 1).

More information about producing a mini-hydro can be obtained from the British Hydropower Association (details below).

Wind power

Wind power harnesses the energy in wind to produce a clean, renewable source of energy without harmful emissions. More and more people in the United Kingdom are interested in generating their own electricity using small-scale wind turbines, and the process is now becoming easier because national planning policies support their development. The cost depends on the type of system you choose, and may range from £1,500–18,000. However, grants of up to £5,000 are offered to individuals and small businesses through the LCBP, and up to £4,000 to people living in Scotland through the Scottish Community and Householder Renewables Initiative (SCHRI). For more information about these schemes, see Appendix 1. Advice about obtaining planning permission, buying equipment and installing a turbine can be obtained from the British Wind Energy Association (details below).

Solar power

There are two main groups of technologies that harness solar power. The first directly converts solar radiation into electricity, most commonly through the use of solar cells, also known as photovoltaic (PV) cells. PV installation may be suitable for properties with a roof or a wall that faces within 90 degrees of south, as long as there is not significant shadow from trees or other buildings. Your roof must be strong enough to take the cells, and you will need to use a fully qualified installer and electrician. Planning permission may be required, especially for listed buildings and in conservation areas. This type of system is a lot more expensive than other solar technologies, but savings can be made on electricity costs over the long term. It may be a suitable option for new buildings or renovation projects where there is no mains electricity available if you have the up-front finances. The cost of installation may range from £5,000–40,000, depending on the wattage required. You will need to seek expert advice to find out whether your property is suitable and whether there is enough sunlight available.

The second group are known as solar thermal technologies, and use the sun to generate heat. In the UK solar heating systems are used to work alongside conventional water heating systems, which cover the winter months when there is not enough heat from the sun. Even so, this type of solar heating system may provide up to two-

Villavent – Europe's favourite domestic ventilation system

Pedigree

Villavent is Europe's leading provider of domestic whole building ventilation systems. These may be in the home, or in larger buildings and complexes such as student and keyworker accommodation, retirement housing and care homes. Villavent is part of a group of companies that operate successfully throughout Europe, the USA and Canada, with an overall turnover in excess of £150 million. Villavent has successfully completed over 100,000 installations, in all types of homes and buildings.

Scandinavian quality and value

Villavent was established over forty years ago and is a bespoke one-stop shop for the design, supply and installation of ventilation systems. Villavent has focused on providing outstanding quality and value for its customers. Scandinavian brilliance can be clearly seen in all our systems, which are designed to be highly energy efficient, quick to install and easy to maintain.

In a cold country, such as Norway, heat conservation is vital. Villavent systems are very energy efficient. Up to 90% of the heat in the outgoing stale air is recovered and used to warm the incoming filtered, fresh air, without the two air streams coming into direct contact with each other. Systems can be further enhanced by the addition of optional cooling systems.

Villavent systems – the most advanced in Europe

Villavent systems are based on the latest technologies and meet all current and planned EU standards, including ISO 9002; the environmental standard, ISO 14001; and the 2006 UK Building Regulations.

Villavent systems are whole building installations, complete with ducts, fittings and grilles. All our systems are supplied with three-dimensional CAD drawings in four colours, full system specifications and a two-year parts guarantee (optional additional 3 year warranty). A UK network of specially appointed and trained Villavent installers is available to provide customers with full installation and maintenance services.

Creating a healthier environment

It is an unfortunate fact that the better our home is insulated, the more likely it is that the air quality will be poor. In Sweden major research has taken place into child health. A study of 9000 families considered the following questions. Are children more allergic if there are pets in the home? What effect does the air quality in our homes have on our children? Do we clean too much? Or too little?

The children were given an extensive medical check-up and their home environments were studied and measured. The study showed a clear relation between low air change rates and high frequency of asthma and allergies.

Villavent heat recovery systems are balanced, meaning they maintain an equilibrium between the volume of dirty, stale, damp air removed from the home and the volume of fresh, filtered, clean air drawn in. With a Villavent system, the air in the house is changed completely. The result is a fresher, healthier living environment.

Villavent filtration dramatically cuts the number of air-borne particles and pollen. This is great news for those who suffer from hay fever and asthma. By lowering the humidity level, Villavent systems help reduce the proliferation of dust mites found in most centrally-heated homes. Dust mites have been linked with a high incidence of asthma among the UK population.

The British Allergy Foundation has formally recognised the significant contribution made by Villavent products in this area by awarding its Seal of Approval.

Villavent – leading a revolution in Heat Recovery Ventilation

Villavent has a range of "revolutionary" Rotary wheel heat exchangers. These meet the demand in the UK for Energy Efficient Healthy Homes (EEHH) and, at the same time, provide a cost effective low energy option for those warm summer months. With AC, and now EC models becoming available and Specific Fan Power (SFP) below the standard rating of 2, Heat Recovery Ventilation from Villavent is indeed very energy efficient.

Villavent Limited
Avenue 2, Station Lane Industrial Estate
Witney, Oxfordshire
OX28 4YL
Tel: 01993 778481   Fax: 01993 772270
E-mail: Sales@villavent.co.uk   Website: www.villavent.co.uk

thirds of a household's annual hot water. Solar panels or collectors, a heat transfer system and a hot water cylinder will be required, and you will need a roof that receives direct sunlight for the main part of the day. It is possible to fit the system yourself if you have the required skills, but grants are not available for DIY projects.

The cost of installation may range from £3,500–7,000, depending on the type of technology you choose, but grants may be available through the LCBP and SCHRI (see Appendix 1). More information about installing solar technologies, including a list of approved installers and suppliers, can be obtained from the EST website or from the British Photovoltaic Association website (www.greenenergy.org. uk/pvuk2).

Geothermal power

Geothermal power is generated by using the heat of the earth, and is considered to be a renewable source of energy if it does not deplete the source of heat. As a homeowner you can use geothermal heat found near the surface of the earth to heat your home directly, or you can use geothermal heat pumps to heat or cool your home indirectly. To install this type of system you would need enough space and the correct conditions to accommodate a trench, borehole or ground loop. Depending on the system you choose, the wattage needed and the groundwork required, the price may range from £6,000–18,000. Grants are available through the LCBP and SCHRI (see Appendix 1). A downloadable factsheet on ground source heat pumps can be obtained from the EST website (see Chapter 1).

Biomass power

Biomass power is generated from burning high-energy plants and organic waste. When plants grow they absorb carbon dioxide which is then released when they are burnt, thus creating a balance that has been called a carbon neutral process. As this is felt to be a neutral process, bio-fuels are considered to be an environmentally sound source of energy, providing new opportunities for UK farmers and a cheaper source of renewable energy for households. There are two ways for a homeowner to use biomass power, either though stand-alone stoves using logs or pellets, or through boilers using pellets, logs or chips. To install this type of system you will need adequate storage space and sufficient air movement space. You will need to comply with safety and building regulations and may need to obtain planning permission for the flue. Costs vary depending on the system you choose, but may be in the region of £1,500–5,000.

Grants are available through the LCBP and SCHRI (see Appendix 1). A downloadable factsheet on biomass can be obtained from the EST website (see Chapter 1).

National schemes for generating energy

There are other types of renewable energy sources that are being developed in the United Kingdom, and, although you cannot harness these sources yourself, you can support research, development and use by investing in green funds and tariffs (see below).

Wave power

Wave power captures the energy produced by ocean surface waves. Although the north and south temperate zones have the best sites for capturing wave power, it has not been a widely used technology in the United Kingdom. At this present time there are only a few experimental sites around the British Isles and storm damage, salt corrosion and prohibitive costs have so far made the technology less commercially viable.

Tidal power

Tidal power harnesses the energy produced by masses of water moving as a result of tides. This makes it a predictable source of renewable energy, unlike other sources that are influenced by fluctuations in the weather. There are several proposals for tidal power schemes in the United Kingdom, but so far the high start-up costs and long payback period have been major stumbling blocks. However, the UK government has acknowledged the importance of tidal power as a renewable source of energy, and it is becoming easier to support research into new technologies through green funds, especially in Scotland.

Landfill gas

As household waste decomposes in landfill sites it gives off methane gas, carbon dioxide and other gases such as hydrogen sulphide. Methane is a potent greenhouse gas and is a danger underground, with the potential to migrate and create an explosive atmosphere. Collecting and converting the gas is seen to be a way to produce renewable energy while reducing the environmental harm it causes.

Waste incineration

Waste incineration, although described as a green energy source by the government, is a controversial way to produce energy as it produces harmful dioxides and means that there may be less encouragement to reuse and recycle. Both Greenpeace and Friends of the Earth believe that refuse cannot provide green energy and that it undermines the development of genuine green technologies. If this is an issue that concerns you, find out whether your current supplier utilizes or supports this type of power generation, and if it does, change supplier.

Green tariffs and green funds

The government has set a target of 10 per cent of electricity production to come from renewable sources by 2010. In order to meet this target, energy suppliers must prove that a proportion of the energy that they sell has come from renewable sources. To do this, suppliers have set up schemes that offer 'green tariffs' or 'green funds' to their customers. These are useful schemes for people who are interested in using renewable energy sources but for whom it is not practical or viable to generate their own electricity.

These schemes offer two ways to use energy from renewable sources supplied by the national grid. First, with most electricity suppliers it is possible to convert to a 'green tariff'. Using this method every unit of electricity that you use is matched by the generation of energy from renewable sources. Second, you may have the option of buying your electricity using a 'green fund'. This uses some of the money from your bill to support research into renewable energy sources, the installation of environmentally friendly technology and other environmental projects.

Changing your supplier or converting to a green tariff will not affect the way that your electricity is supplied or the way that you are billed. However, the availability, quality and price of green tariffs and green funds vary significantly across the country so you need to shop around for the best deal. The Green Electricity Marketplace provides a useful guide to green tariffs and green funds in the United Kingdom (details below), or visit www.uswitch.com for a useful comparison of all suppliers in your area.

Reusing and recycling

Waste and recycling methods and collections vary across the United Kingdom, with some local authorities having much more developed systems than others. The easiest way to recycle your waste is to make use of your local authority collection and recycling services. Contact the authority direct to find out what services are available, and for advice about what waste can be recycled in your area. Information about composting and recycling green waste and water is provided in Chapter 11.

Paper

One of the best ways to reduce paper waste is to stop receiving junk mail. Contact the Mailing Preference Service to get your name removed from mailing lists (tel: 020 7291 3310; website: www.mpsonline.org.uk). Most types of paper are now accepted for recycling, and it usually takes three to four weeks for recycled paper to reappear on the market in the form of newspapers and other recycled paper. However, you may find that Yellow Pages cannot be accepted for normal recycling in your area as the dye is not suitable. Instead, local authorities arrange separate collections and the books can be recycled into products like animal bedding, padded envelopes and house insulation. Alternatively, you can find out whether your child's school is involved in the Yellow Woods Challenge. This is a scheme that encourages children to recycle Yellow Pages (www.yellow-woods.co.uk).

Some local authorities will not accept shredded paper because some paper mills will not take it – this is because the paper fibres have been weakened, and the equipment may be unsuitable so that the shreds cause maintenance problems or create a fire hazard. Contact your local authority for more information. If it does not accept shredded paper it should be able to recommend a local company that will dispose of it safely.

Cardboard

Cardboard is made from cellulose fibres, usually from wood pulp, and can be recycled, although because of its lightweight and low quality it is not collected by some local authorities. You can use cardboard in your own garden for compost and mulch (see Chapter 11) or you can use the search facility at www.recyclenow.com to find your nearest cardboard recycling centre. All cardboard that is to be sent for recycling should be made as flat as possible, and adhesives and fasteners should be removed.

Plastic

Plastic is damaging to the environment, both in the way it is manufactured as it uses petrochemicals and high-temperature furnaces, and in the way that it cannot break down naturally. It is important to encourage retailers and manufacturers to use less plastic and to try to buy products supplied in other types of container. At present it tends to be only the 'bottle' type of plastic that can be recycled, such as drink, shampoo and cleaning bottles. Recycled plastic is not reused for food and drink but instead is made into items such as furniture, drainage pipes and fleece for outdoor clothing. Bottles should be washed and squashed, with tops removed.

Glass

EU law will soon require the UK to recycle 70 per cent of its glass. Most types of glass can be recycled and it can be reused over and over again. The only types of glass that cannot be recycled are certain types of toughened glass, window panes, glass ovenware, light bulbs and some types of ornamental glass. If using bottle banks you must sort using the correct colours as the quality of recycled material can be affected, and all bottles should be rinsed, with caps and lids removed. Recycled glass is crushed, melted and moulded to make new bottles and jars, or can be used as aggregate in road building.

Cans

Food and drink cans should be washed before recycling, as contamination can disrupt the smelting process. The cans should be crushed although labels need not be removed. Steel cans are separated from aluminium cans using a large magnet. Impure steel is reused for road building and pure steel is reused for cans, car parts and domestic appliances.

Aluminium foil

To find out whether something is made of aluminium foil, crush it in your hand. Aluminium foil will stay crushed whereas silver-coated plastic materials will spring back. All foil should be washed and kept separate from other recycling materials. It is recycled into more foil or items such as lightweight car parts.

Clothes, shoes and textiles

Items in good condition can be sent to charity shops or bagged up for collection. Pairs of shoes should be tied together, and items should not be damp or dirty as this can contaminate whole batches. Poorer quality items can be recycled for certain types of fillings, and gradually more local authorities are setting up such schemes. Contact your authority direct to find out what schemes are available in your area, or use the postcode locator at www.recyclenow.com to find your nearest collection point. Recently there has been considerable media coverage about bogus charity clothes collectors, so make sure that you only use legitimate collection points and/or charitable groups.

Spectacles

Vision Aid Overseas collects donated spectacles from opticians' practices in the United Kingdom to deliver to its offices all over the world to help people with poor eyesight. Contact your optician to find out whether it takes part in the scheme. If not, more information about donating spectacles can be obtained from Vision Aid Overseas (tel: 01293 535 016; website: www.vao.org.uk). Some Help the Aged shops will also accept unwanted pairs of glasses.

Nappies

The problems associated with disposable nappies have been well highlighted in recent years. Where possible, parents should only use real (reusable cloth) nappies. To obtain details about real nappy retailers, networks, laundries and incentive schemes in the United Kingdom, contact the Real Nappy Campaign (tel: 0845 850 0606; website: www.realnappycampaign.com). (If you live in Wales, tel: 0845 456 2477; website: www.realnappies-wales.org.uk.)

Computers

Contact your local authority to find out what schemes are available for recycling old computers. Alternatively, you can donate your PC to a needy organization (www.donateapc.org.uk) or use the Freecycle Network to give away old equipment (www.freecycle.org). Before sending your computer for recycling, make sure that you use a specialist software package to wipe clean your hard drive. This involves much more than file deletion or simple reformatting, and if you are unsure of what you are doing you should seek specialist advice. Personal data theft from discarded hard drives is becoming an increasingly common problem.

Engine oil

Most engine oil can be disposed of through local authority household waste recycling centres. Make sure that it is not mixed with other substances and that it is stored in a sealed container. If you have a large amount of oil to dispose of, or if you need more advice about getting rid of engine oil, contact the Environment Agency oil care campaign (tel: 08708 506 506; website: www.oilbankline.org.uk). You can find your nearest oil bank by using the search facility on this website.

Car batteries

By law, car batteries must not be disposed of as general household waste. Instead, you must use the specialist facility at your local authority household waste recycling centre, or ask your battery supplier to dispose of the old battery safely. From the batteries, the lead, plastic and distilled water is recycled and the acid is treated and neutralized.

Furniture and appliances

Donate furniture to local charity shops, hostels, youth centres or church groups. Many will come to collect unwanted items. Alternatively, you can contact the furniture reuse network for information and help on recycling furniture and appliances (www.frn.org.uk).

This organization is a national coordinating body for furniture and appliance reuse and recycling organizations in the United Kingdom, which collect a wide range of household items to pass onto people in need.

Knowing about grants and discount schemes

There are a variety of grants and discount schemes for homeowners who want their home to become more energy efficient and live a more environmentally friendly life. More information about all these schemes is provided in Appendix 1.

The Home Energy Efficiency Scheme (Wales)

This scheme is available for homeowners and tenants who live in Wales. It is aimed primarily at households with the greatest health risks – older people, people with children under the age of 16 and people who are disabled and chronically sick. Through this scheme a grant of up to £2,700 is provided to make homes warmer, more energy efficient and more secure.

Warm Front (England)

Warm Front was launched in June 2000 as the Home Energy Efficiency Scheme. Through this scheme a grant of £2,700 or £4,000 (if oil central heating has been recommended) is available to certain households in England. To qualify for the scheme you must own your own home or rent from a private landlord, have a child under 16 or be at least 26 weeks pregnant, and be in receipt of state benefits.

Warm Deal (Scotland)

This scheme provides grants of up to £500, which can be put towards a number of energy-saving measures for certain households in Scotland. To be eligible for the scheme you or your spouse must own or rent your home, be over the age of 60 or be in receipt of state benefits. The grant will help to pay for cavity wall, loft, pipe or tank insulation, draught-proofing and energy-efficient lighting.

Central Heating Programme (Scotland)

This scheme helps certain household in Scotland to improve the heating systems in their home. To qualify for the scheme you must be resident in Scotland and own or rent your home, which must be your main or only residence. The property should not have a central heating system, or the present system should be broken beyond repair, and you will need to have lived in the property for at least 12 months and intend to live in the property for at least 12 months once the heating system has been installed.

Warm Homes (Northern Ireland)

Through this scheme grants of up to £750 are provided for home-owners and tenants in Northern Ireland who are in receipt of certain benefits.

Low Carbon Buildings Programme

Through the Low Carbon Buildings Programme individual house-holders can apply for grants to help with the installation of renewable sources of energy for their homes. Larger grants are available for communities who decide to install renewable energy technology for community use.

Scottish Community and Householder Renewables Initiative

The Scottish Community and Householder Renewables Initiative offers grants and advice to people in Scotland who wish to develop renewable sources of energy. To qualify for a grant you must own the property where the renewable energy system is to be installed, you must obtain a quotation from an accredited installer and you must use an approved installer using an approved system.

The Energy Efficiency Commitment

In the United Kingdom the government requires energy companies to fund energy improvements in domestic homes. Under the Energy

Efficiency Commitment (EEC), companies are obliged to provide grants for home owners to install cavity wall and loft insulation. At the time of writing the grant provides a £200 discount for cavity wall insulation and £150 for loft insulation. These grants are changing constantly, so for the most up-to-date information consult your local authority or your local Energy Efficiency Advice Centre.

Renovation grants

Renovation grants are designed to help owner-occupiers carry out repairs or improvements to their properties, and some local authorities enable you to include energy-efficiency improvements in the works. In most cases these grants are discretionary and depend on the amount of funds available. To obtain a grant you will need to hold the freehold and intend to live in or let the property for a specified number of years. Your property will need to have been classed 'unfit' for habitation or have failed the new Housing Health and Safety Rating System (HHSRS) assessment. Contact your local authority for more information about this grant.

Summary

There are many changes that you, as a homeowner, can make to move towards a more environmentally friendly way of living. These include making changes to the way you use energy and buy energy-using products, converting to renewable forms of energy, and reusing and recycling. There are a variety of grants and discount schemes available for people interested in making these changes to their current home.

In some cases it may be preferable to think about buying a greener property or purchasing a property that is more suited to making environmentally friendly changes. If you decide that this is a preferable option, advice and information about buying a green property is offered in the next chapter.

Useful organizations

National Association of Loft Insulation Contractors (NALIC)

NALIC represents the loft insulation contracting industry and its suppliers. It can provide information about loft insulation and a list of members in your area.

National Association of Loft Insulation Contractors
PO Box 12
Haslemere
Surrey GU27 3AH
Tel: 01428 654 011
Fax: 01428 651 401

Cavity Insulation Guarantee Agency (CIGA)

CIGA is an independent agency that provides independent 25-year guarantees for cavity wall insulation fitted by registered installers. The guarantee covers materials and workmanship, and is available to subsequent owners of the property. CIGA will investigate complaints, and where necessary, ensure that remedial work is carried out free of charge.

Cavity Insulation Guarantee Agency
CIGA House, 3 Vimy Court
Vimy Road
Leighton Buzzard
Bedfordshire LU7 1FG
Tel: 01525 853 300
Fax: 01525 385 926
E-mail: info@cigaco.uk
Website: www.ciga.co.uk

British Fenestration Rating Council (BFRC)

BFRC has developed and operates a UK national rating system for the thermal performance of fenestration products. On the website you can search for the best performing windows in terms of energy efficiency, and search for an installer, manufacturer and supplier of energy-saving windows.

British Fenestration Rating Council Ltd
44–48 Borough High Street
London SE1 1XB
Tel: 020 7403 9200
Fax: 0870 042 4266
E-mail: info@bfrc.org
Website: www.brfc.org

Renewable Energy Association

The Renewable Energy Association is the trade body for renewable energy producers in the United Kingdom. Although it is unable to provide answers to specific queries from members of the public, its website contains useful and detailed information about all types of renewable energy, and you can search its database for a member in your area.

Renewable Energy Association
17 Waterloo Place
London SW1Y 4AR
Tel: 020 7747 1830
Fax: 020 7925 2715
E-mail: use enquiry form on website
Website: www.r-e-a.net

Centre for Alternative Technology (CAT)

CAT is a charity concerned with tackling the serious issues that face our planet such as climate change, pollution and the waste of precious resources. Its visitor centre is situated in southern Snowdonia, and you can see displays highlighting the power of wind, water and sun, and visit working examples of environmentally responsible buildings, energy conservation, organic growing and composting. CAT produces a variety of leaflets on issues such as green tariffs, home heating with renewable energy, environmental building, investing in renewable energy, small-scale wind power, water harvesting and reusing grey water.

Centre for Alternative Technology
Machynlleth
Powys SY20 9AZ
Tel: 01654 705 950
Fax: 01654 702 782
Website: www.cat.org.uk

British Wind Energy Association (BWEA)

BWEA is the trade and professional body for the wind and marine renewables industries. The primary aim of the association is to promote the use of wind power around the United Kingdom, both inshore and offshore. If you are interested in installing your own wind turbine you can obtain an information pack and a list of small wind turbine suppliers from the BWEA.

British Wind Energy Association
Renewable Energy House
1 Aztec Row, Berners Road
London N1 0PW
Tel: 020 7689 1960
Fax: 020 7689 1969
E-mail: info@bwea.com
Website: www.bwea.com

Useful websites

www.nationalinsulationassociation.org.uk
The National Insulation Association (NIA) represents the manufacturers and installers of all types of insulation and draught-proofing. On this website you can find details of an installer and manufacturer in your area by accessing the Register of Members and the Register of Manufacturers. The website contains useful information about insulation and draught-proofing techniques and materials.

www.centralheating.co.uk
This is the website of the Heating and Hot Water Industry Council (HHIC). It is an independent organization which aims to provide unbiased information on all heating and hot water matters. On its website you can find information about saving energy and grants,

find a registered installer and order a heat loss calculator. This is an accurate and simple programme that helps you to calculate how much heat is being lost in your home.

www.greenelectricity.org
This is the website of the Green Electricity Marketplace. You can select the region in which you live or to which you want to move to find out about the local suppliers that offer green tariffs. Prices and services are compared, along with useful information about choosing a suitable supplier and advice about the different types of renewable energy sources.

www.british-hydro.org
The British Hydropower Association represents the interests of people who are involved in the production of hydro power in the United Kingdom, from large companies to individuals and charities. On its website you can find comprehensive information about producing hydro power and the costs involved.

www.lowcaronbuildings.org.uk
This is the website of the Low Carbon Buildings Programme. On this site you can find information about grants available for the installation of renewable energy technologies.

Further reading

Roberts, J (2003) *Good Green Homes*, Gibbs M Smith, Layton, Utah
Scott, N (2004) *Reduce, Reuse, Recycle! An easy household guide*, Green Books, Totnes
Smith, P (2003) *Eco-Refurbishment: A practical guide to creating an energy efficient home*, Architectural Press, Oxford

3 Home-buyers

If you are thinking about buying a property in which to live or for investment purposes, you have more potential scope to find a place that meets your green philosophy. This is because you can take your time to search for the right property that already matches your green philosophy, or one that you can refurbish, renovate or convert in a way that suits your environmental and ethical wishes.

When searching for a new property you should use your green code as discussed in Chapter 1 to help you to produce a checklist that will enable you to narrow your search for suitable properties. Once you have done this you need to find suitable properties, understand how to recognize the green potential of a property, evaluate the potential for the installation of renewable energy sources, know what to avoid, understand the costs involved, and arrange suitable building and contents insurance for your new property. This chapter provides advice and guidance about all these issues.

Developing a green checklist

When you begin your search for an environmentally friendly property it is useful to develop a property-hunting checklist that you can use to match your environmental, financial and personal criteria against the properties in which you are interested. This checklist will help you to narrow down your choice of suitable properties, and enable you to ask the right questions of estate agents and vendors while making sure that the property meets your criteria during viewing.

Your checklist will depend on your personal green code, your financial situation and your personal wants and needs (see Chapter 1), and may include some or all of the issues listed below:

■ How much do you want to pay for the property? Are you willing to pay more for a greener property?

■ How many bedrooms and reception rooms do you require?

■ What size garden do you require? Are you interested in growing your own food? Are the soil type, drainage, geology and topography suitable for your needs? Is the garden south-facing without significant shadow?

■ What fixtures and fittings are included in the purchase price? Some people take everything they can with them when they move, including light bulbs, so this might provide an opportunity to start replacing fixtures and fittings with energy-efficient alternatives.

■ Which energy supplier is presently used in the property? If you are not thinking about installing your own source of energy, consider green tariffs (see Chapter 2). You can check whether it is possible to sign up to a green tariff for the property in which you are interested by consulting www.greenelectricity.org.

■ What is the standard of the present gas boiler? Does it need replacing? If so, you could try to negotiate a reduction on the asking price and then install a high-efficiency condensing boiler. For independent, professional advice about heating consult the Heating and Hot Water Industry Council (www.centralheating. co.uk).

■ What heating controls are already installed? These could include a central heating and domestic hot water timer, a programmable room thermostat, a hot water thermostat and thermostatic radiator valves. You may be able to negotiate on the price if you need to replace any heating controls.

■ Does the house have higher than normal levels of insulation? Have environmentally friendly products been used? Ask about lofts, pipes, walls, floors, doors and windows. Where possible, ask to see loft insulation and check that it has a depth of at least 270 millimetres. Find out whether there are any guarantees covering wall insulation (see Chapter 2).

■ What is the standard and layout of glazing? Are there larger amounts of glazing facing south, to maximize light and warmth, and smaller amounts to the north elevations? Generally, is there plenty of glazing to maximize daylight and take advantage of the heat from the sun?

■ What natural materials have been used in the building? This may include a timber frame, wool insulation, straw bale walls and environmentally friendly paints.

Build & Protect, for all our tomorrows

ECOLOGICAL BUILDING SYSTEMS

LOW-ENERGY INTELLIGENT BUILDING SOLUTIONS

www.ecologicalbuildingsystems.co.uk

Infiltration and uncontrolled ventilation can account for up to 50% of heat loss in modern homes & increased CO_2 emissions

It has long been established that ventilation is an absolute & essential part of creating a healthy, comfortable, energy efficient home. Unfortunately, air leakage and uncontrolled ventilation means that expensive heated air escapes from our homes, wasting valuable energy. This energy leakage is one of the most significant contributors to inefficiently heated homes and can account for up to 50% of heat loss in modern homes while also leading to a reduction in the durability & viability of the structure.

Airtightness and Natural Insulation

Research has shown that approximately 40% of the energy consumed in the UK goes into the servicing of buildings, of which 60% is used for water/space heating and cooling.

In the past the majority of heat loss through the fabric of the building envelope was as a result of little or no insulation and a very low level of draught sealing (Airtightness). The most cost effective means of reducing heating bills, increasing the energy efficiency in homes and ensuring that the insulation can work to 100% of its ability, is to use a quality insulation while making sure the structure is Airtight.

THERMO-HEMP is made from Hemp and is pollutant-FREE, ruling out any health risk either in production, installation or use. Thermo-Hemp provides a totally natural, healthy, comfortable living atmosphere. It has an ability to absorb & release moisture and is not affected by mould growth or insect attack. It is dust-free causing no irritation and is easy to handle & convenient to install. Used in conjunction with the pro clima Airtight System it provides a perfect partnership for reduced energy bills, reduced carbon emissions, while creating a natural, healthy living environment.

Airtight, Air-Right

The **pro clima Airtight System** utilises an intelligent membrane, that manages the inherent moisture, which may otherwise become trapped within the structural elements, even after the building is complete.

pro clima for Intelligent Moisture Management in Structural Elements

Active Moisture Management, Structural Protection & Energy Efficiency

This system combines intelligent Vapour Checks which are humidity variable and vapour permeable (e.g. pro clima INTELLOplus) and a range of non-toxic specialist tapes (designed for every construction detail), adhesives and sealing solutions to ensure a building is airtight and healthy.

High Performing Intelligent Vapour Check, Energy Savings & Moisture Management

INTELLOplus Vapour Check controls the moisture which may become trapped within the structural elements, even after the building is complete. In winter months it acts as an effective Vapour Check protecting the structure against warm moist air diffusing through, while in summer, INTELLOplus reduces its resistance to vapour transfer by up to 50 times allowing rapid back drying to the inside.

At What Cost?

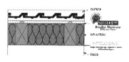

Intelligent Airtightness, can be achieved at a fraction of one precent of the total build cost and allows for significant savings to be made on energy costs and potential structural repairs. A sufficiently Airtight home is also the only way that insulation and the heating system can actually work to 100% of its ability.

By Niall Crosson (MEng Sc, BTech, MIEI) Technical Engineer
Contact: Ecological Building Systems UK Ltd, The Manse, High Street, Creaton, Northants, NN6 8NA
 Mail: ecologicalbuild@btconnect.com
 Tel: 05600 758025
 Fax: 05600 758026
 Web: www.ecologicalbuildingsystems.co.uk

Natural Thermal & Acoustic Hemp Insulation

pro clima
Intelligent Airtight Systems
airtight air-right

■ Does the property have a grey-water collection system for watering the garden, or the potential for developing one? You may need to install a tank, pump and additional pipes so you will need to make sure there is enough space available.

■ Does the property have a rainwater harvesting system, or the potential to develop one? This will include space for a tank, pump and filter, and may require pipe and gutter replacement.

■ If you are interested in composting toilets, is there potential to build one? Is there enough private space available in the garden? Is the property overlooked?

■ Is the property located in a conservation area or is it a listed building? Would planning permission be granted for any changes you may wish to make?

■ Are there any neighbours living close by who might object to your green plans? Are there are any shared rights of way or issues with boundaries that could create problems (see Chapter 9)?

■ Is the location of the property suitable for your green plans? Is the area windy and/or sunny enough for your proposed energy schemes? Are there good local authority recycling schemes available? Are there efficient and cheap suppliers of fuel, organic food, plants and seeds? Is there local access to reclamation yards and retailers supplying local goods and produce?

Finding suitable properties

Once you have developed your green checklist you can start to hunt for suitable properties. Your checklist should help you to narrow your search, especially if you have been quite specific about your property requirements. It is possible to e-mail, deliver or post your checklist to estate agents in the locality in which you are interested, but be prepared to receive information about all sorts of properties, most of which will not match your criteria.

If you intend to e-mail your information to estate agents, you might find it useful to set up a separate e-mail account as you may be inundated with responses that could clog up your inbox. UK Property Matters (www.ukpropertymatters.co.uk) is a useful website that enables you to send your details to all estate agents in a specified area. You can also specify your green criteria in an additional information box, although again, you should not expect all estate agents to take too much notice of these criteria. If you use this service, don't be tempted to tick too many counties as you will be flooded with property details. GreenMoves is a useful organization for people interested in hunting specifically for more energy-efficient homes (details below).

Once you have found a property in which you are interested, you can obtain useful statistics about the area by consulting the Neighbourhood Statistics website (details below). This website will provide information about population, crime, health and housing in the area. More information about the property and its boundaries can be obtained from the Land Registry website (England and Wales) and the Registers of Scotland Executive Agency (Scotland) (details below).

Recognizing and evaluating green potential

If you do not have a lot of money to spend on making green improvements to a new property, it makes sense to buy a property that already has a high green rating. From June 2007 the easiest way to do this will be to take note of the energy performance certificate (EPC) which will be produced as part of the home information pack (see Chapter 4). It is also possible to obtain an independent energy audit for the property in which you are interested. If you find that the property does not rate highly on the audit you can think about moving on to another property, or you can negotiate with the vendors to reduce the price in light of the audit. You can find a building surveyor experienced in conducting an energy audit by consulting the RICS database (www.ricsfirms.com). Alternatively, contact your local authority as some are now providing a free or reduced-fee energy audit for local households. Some local energy suppliers will also conduct a free energy audit, and the Co-operative Bank will provide a free home energy report with your mortgage valuation.

Question vendors carefully about the EPC and the independent audit, if you have obtained one, making sure that the property meets the criteria listed in your green checklist. Vendors who have purposively developed a green property should be able to answer your specific questions in detail, especially if they are very enthusiastic about the green credentials of their property. If you are interested in their property ask them to explain and demonstrate the environmentally friendly systems and schemes they have in place so that you can find out whether they would meet your needs and match your green code. You may also find it useful to obtain an

ɔːDimplex ®

GO FOR GREEN WITH DIMPLEX HEAT PUMPS

Dimplex heat pumps are the environmentally friendly answer to increasingly expensive energy supplies, offering you a sustainable heating solution which will help the environment and save you money.

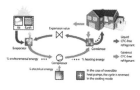

A Dimplex heat pump draws heat from the environment and compresses it to heat a building

Heat pumps extract inexhaustible, freely available heat from the ground or air and compress it to provide highly efficient, economical heating. Although the technology is fairly new to the UK, heat pumps have been used in Europe for many years. Dimplex has over 25 years' manufacturing experience and there are thousands of Dimplex heat pumps installed across Europe.

Ground source heat pumps, which extract heat from the ground through buried collectors, are generally better known in this country, but air source (or 'air-to-water') heat pumps are likely to become the technology of choice in the UK. As the name suggests, air-to-water heat pumps use the ambient air as their source of heat. This means that unlike ground source heat pumps they don't have the cost or space requirement of installing ground collectors, which makes them more practical and cost-effective in many applications, both new-build and retro-fit.

Air source is ideal for mild climates

Already out-selling ground source heat pumps in countries such as

Germany and France, air source technology is ideally suited to the British climate with its comparatively mild winters. While Dimplex air-to-water heat pumps can collect heat from the air at temperatures as low as -20 degrees Celsius, above 0 degrees Celsius the efficiency improves dramatically. With the average winter temperature in the UK being around 4 degrees Celsius, an average co-efficient of performance of 3.4-4 can be expected. While this may be lower than ground source heat pumps in some cases, total installation costs are obviously lower. Because they don't require collectors, another benefit of air source heat pumps is that there is minimum disturbance to the site, making air-to-water heat pumps ideal for refurbishment applications, particularly where space is limited.

An air source heat pump is normally specified to meet all the heating and hot water requirements for a property, down to at least 0 degrees Celsius. At lower temperatures the heat pump is automatically supplemented by an electric immersion heater, but in more typical temperatures, the only running cost is the electrical energy needed to run the heat pump's compressor.

Because they don't require collectors, air source heat pumps mean minimum disturbance to the site

Dimplex offers an extensive range of air source heat pumps which are designed for either outdoor or indoor installation to give complete flexibility for the homeowner, and models are available with heating capacities from 5-28kW. 'Reversible' models with both heating and cooling capabilities are also available.

In addition to its own fully trained staff who can offer advice on what size and type of heat pump is required, Dimplex has a network of installer partners who are able to provide pre-installation site visits, full installation, commissioning and after-sales support service.

Take it for granted

At the time of writing, there are a number of grant schemes in operation which support individuals and organisations wanting to install heat pumps. In Scotland, air source heat pumps have been accredited under the Scottish Communities and Householder Renewables Initiative (SCHRI), making them eligible for grants of up to £4000 per installation. The scheme provides grants to individual householders, community groups and housing developers for the installation of heat pumps and other microgeneration technologies.

Dimplex offers air source models for both outdoor and indoor installation

In addition, throughout the UK, the Low Carbon Buildings Programme (LCBP) is due to accredit air source heat pumps for grant funding during spring/summer 2007. This scheme offers grants for microgeneration technologies to householders, community groups and public sector bodies, and previously only awarded grants for ground source heat pumps. For more details on these grant schemes, visit **www.dimplex-resource.co.uk** or **www.dti.gov.uk**

Heat pumps make the best use of nature's energy to give reliable, secure, inflation-proof heating. With air-to-water heat pumps so well suited to our climate and so easy to install in a wide variety of applications, and with the grant support now available, air source technology is set to become very widely adopted in the UK.

Dimplex   Tel: 01489 773336   Fax: 01489 773061
email: marketing@glendimplex.com or www.dimplex.co.uk

alternative energy assessment (see below) to help you to recognize and evaluate the green potential of the property.

Recognizing potential for renewable energy sources

The different types of renewable energy source are discussed in Chapter 2. If you are looking for a new property and you want to install sources of renewable energy, you need to look out for additional features within the property and grounds. These include the following issues:

■ Is the house correctly orientated for solar panels? Take a compass with you to make sure that it faces within 90 degrees of south and that there are no buildings and trees creating shadow on the place where the panels would be located. Would there be enough sunlight or heat to effectively harness solar power? You may need to seek independent, professional advice. Is the roof in good condition and strong enough to take the panels? Is there room for an additional water cylinder, if required? Will planning permission be granted? Check with the local planning authority prior to making your purchase. More information about solar heating can be obtained from the British Photovoltaic Association website (www.greenernergy.org.uk/pvuk2).

■ Is the ground suitable for a geothermal system? Is there space available for a trench or borehole? What type of heating distribution system is already installed in the property? You can use existing radiators, but underfloor heating tends to be more effective.

■ Is it possible to install a wood-fired central heating system? Does the property have the space available for storage, and is there a local fuel supplier available? Is the chimney suitable? Is the property located in a smokeless zone? If this is the case you can only burn wood on exempted appliances under the Clean Air Act. You will need to seek advice about obtaining planning permission for the installation of the flue.

■ Is there space and enough height to install a wind turbine? To obtain an estimate of wind speeds in the area of the property, consult the UK Wind Speed Database on the British Wind Energy Association website (www.bwea.com). Would planning permission be granted? Seek advice from the local planning authority before making your purchase.

▌ Is there a suitable source of water close to the property, with the required level of flow and height for a mini-hydro scheme, or the possibility of managing the flow and height to meet your requirements? Will your water management have an adverse influence on the ecology of the river? Will you be able to obtain planning permission for your mini-hydro plant? More information about producing a mini-hydro can be obtained from the British Hydro Association (www.british-hydro.org).

Obtaining an alternative energy assessment

If you feel that you do not have the required expertise to assess the potential for alternative energy sources on a property that you have found, it is possible to obtain an assessment from an experienced individual or company. The Energy Alternatives website (www. energyalteratives.co.uk) has been set up by a couple who found it hard to obtain independent advice about alternative technologies. Now they offer free generic advice to households or tailored, no-obligation assessments for a small fee. They can also put you in touch with reliable installers and offer information about grants. Consult the website for more information about the service.

If you are interested in a specific type of renewable energy you can contact the relevant trade association to find a reputable installer and/or manufacturer (see useful organizations at the end of this book). These people will be able to offer a no-obligation assessment of the property for the suitability of their alternative technology.

Avoiding unsuitable properties

If you are hoping to buy a property that is suitable for your family home and meets your green philosophy, think about avoiding the following types of property:

▌ Properties that require too much work and expense to make them habitable and enable them to meet your green requirements.

▌ Houses in an area that is unsuitable for your family. This may be an area of degeneration where properties are losing their value and there are local problems with crime, vandalism and burglaries, or it may be an area where the climatic conditions and topography are not suitable to sustain your green way of life.

■ Properties located near noisy, dangerous roads, airports or railway lines. Although you and your family may be able to put up with the noise and inconvenience, you may find it difficult to sell your property when you wish to move on. Also, you need to consider issues of pollution – high levels of pollution will not suit your green lifestyle.

■ Houses that have been built and decorated using harmful and non-sustainable materials and products. While it may be possible to refurbish and renovate using your green criteria, you should make sure that the costs and work involved are not prohibitive.

■ Properties located in areas where it is not suitable to install renewable energy technologies. You can have an independent assessment carried out to determine suitability (see above).

If you are hoping to carry out significant work to improve the green credentials of your new property, there are certain types of property that you should avoid buying, as your development plans may be restricted, curtailed or denied. These include listed buildings, properties in sensitive areas and properties that contain restrictive covenants in their title deeds. More information about knowing what to avoid when buying a property for development is provided in Chapter 9.

Knowing about the costs

As a potential purchaser you need to work out how much you are able to afford and how much extra you are willing to pay for a green property. If you are hoping to develop or make a profit from your property, think about buying cheaply and making alterations that will add value without costing a lot of money. It is important to start taking notice of what is happening with property prices in your area or in the area in which you are interested. Monitor the prices and keep a record – this will help you to see how prices are changing in both the short and long term. Regularly visit local estate agents and consult the local property press, again keeping records so that you can monitor changes.

The Land Registry produces a *Residential Property Price Report* which provides a detailed insight into what is happening to average prices and sales volumes in the residential property market for England and Wales. This is useful on both a national and local level to get an up-to-date idea of house prices and sales. The information is freely available on the website (details below). A similar survey is produced in Scotland by the Registers of Scotland Executive Agency (details below).

In addition to this research you need to find out about the prices of environmentally friendly properties. The GreenMoves website provides a useful starting point for your research, but you can also contact local estate agents and ask them to keep you informed of environmentally friendly properties that come on the market. Visit these properties to compare prices, features, facilities, style and level of eco-friendliness.

When buying an eco-friendly property, or a property that you wish to develop in an environmentally friendly way, there are various other costs that you need to consider. These include initial costs associated with the purchase and the costs associated with the development of the property. The following list provides an example of the costs that may be involved.

Initial purchase costs

Solicitor's fees:	£600–1,000
Search fees:	£70–250
Conveyancing fees:	£300–500
Surveyor's fees:	£400–800
Stamp Duty Land Tax:	1–4 per cent of the purchase price
Mortgage broker fee:	£100–200
Mortgage booking fee:	£100–500
Valuation fee:	£125–500
Re-inspection fee:	£50–200
Deposit:	variable
Purchase price:	variable

Development costs

Eco-friendly paint/wallpaper:	£50–800
Eco-friendly fixtures and fittings:	£500–5,000
Eco-friendly furnishings:	£500–5,000
Buildings and contents insurance:	£150–400
Labour:	variable
Equipment:	variable
Plant and tool hire:	variable

Information about the costs of installing renewable energy technologies and energy-efficiency measures is provided in Chapters 2 and 4. To be able to plan your budget successfully you must be aware of all the costs involved at the beginning of your project, and all quotations must be obtained well in advance. This includes the fees of professionals, taxes, mortgage fees, building work and materials, fixtures, fittings, furniture and decoration. Even the most carefully planned budget may require extra funding, so it is a good idea to provide around 15 per cent of your total budget as a contingency fund to cover unexpected expenses.

Electronic conveyancing

The Land Registration Act 2002 sets out the new legislation for the implementation of e-conveyancing services. It is intended that this new electronic conveyancing system will make the process of buying and selling property easier for homeowners and professionals. The system should enable authorized parties to obtain and send information much quicker, transfer funds immediately and update property and related information as soon as it is required. It is hoped that e-conveyancing will be introduced in 2007 when the new home information packs come into force. However, there are many concerns about the system, in particular whether the conveyancing process will be cheaper for homeowners, the amount of public/professional access to the information, how it is stored and whether the system might fail. More information about this new system can be obtained from the Land Registry website (www.landreg.gov.uk).

Arranging green building and contents insurance

Once you have made an offer on a property you need to look into arranging building and contents insurance. This insurance is compulsory when you take out a mortgage but you do not have to take out this cover with your mortgage lender, although some might charge an administration fee if you decide to use another company. Some lenders may attach this cover to their more attractive mortgages, so you should check this when arranging your loan. However, if this is the case you may not be able to choose ethical or green insurance. Today there are a small number of companies that offer green types of insurance, so you should shop around for a company that matches your ethical criteria.

Naturesave Policies Ltd provides buildings and content insurance for homeowners who are interested in environmental issues. Ten per cent of the premium generated from the sale of all policies is put into a charitable trust that has been established to benefit environmental and conservationist organizations on specific projects. More information about its policies can be obtained from its website or by telephone (tel: 01803 864 390; website: www.natursave.co.uk). Co-operative Insurance also provides the opportunity to take out buildings and contents insurance from a company that operates under a strict ethical code. More information about its policies can be obtained from the website (www.cis.co.uk).

Summary

When buying a new property you have more scope for finding a house that matches your green philosophy or a house that has the potential to be renovated or converted in a way that suits your green wishes. It is important to develop a checklist which will help you to know what to look for and the questions to ask when viewing a property. It is also important to know what type of properties to avoid, as it may be difficult or expensive to make green improvements, or you may find it difficult to sell your property when it is time to move.

Good green credentials can add value to a property, and you may have to be prepared to spend a little more on a property that already has many green features. However, this can work in your favour when you come to sell your own green property, as potential buyers may be willing to spend more for a property that meets their green requirements. These issues are discussed in the following chapter.

Useful organizations

The Department for Communities and Local Government (DCLG)

DCLG was created on 5 May 2006 under the leadership of Ruth Kelly. You can obtain information about the new home information pack, along with other useful housing information, from the DCLG.

Department for Communities and Local Government
Eland House, Bressenden Place
London SW1E 5DU
Tel: 020 7944 4400
Fax: 020 7944 9645
E-mail: contactus@communities.gsi.gov.uk
Website: www.communities.gov.uk

Association of Home Information Pack Providers (AHIPP)

AHIPP was founded in June 2005 to represent people and organizations involved in the production and preparation of home information packs. On its website you can obtain information about what the organization does, along with links to organizations providing home information pack services.

Association of Home Information Pack Providers
3 Savile Row
London W1S 3PB
Tel: 0870 950 7739
Fax: 01858 454 714
E-mail: info@hipassociation.co.uk
Website: www.hipassociation.co.uk

Royal Institute of Chartered Surveyors (RICS)

RICS is the largest organization for professionals working in property, land and construction worldwide. RICS members have to adhere to a strict code of conduct and are required to update their skills and knowledge on a regular basis. All members must have proper insurance, and customers are protected by a RICS formal complaints service.

Royal Institute of Chartered Surveyors
RICS Contact Centre
Surveyor Court, Westwood Way
Coventry CV4 8JE
Tel: 0870 333 1600
Fax: 020 7334 3811
E-mail: contactrics@rics.org
Website: www.rics.org

Council of Licensed Conveyancers

The Council of Licensed Conveyancers is the regulatory body for licensed conveyancers, who are qualified specialist property lawyers. You can obtain the contact details of a conveyancer in your area by using the online directory.

Council of Licensed Conveyancers
16 Glebe Road
Chelmsford
Essex CM1 1QG
Tel: 01245 349599
Fax: 01245 341300
Website: www.theclc.gov.uk

Useful websites

www.neighbourhood.statistics.gov.uk
You can find statistics for local areas on a wide range of subjects which include population, crime, health and housing on this site. By entering the postcode of the property in which you are interested you can obtain summary statistics of the area based on the 2001 Census. A useful table shows you the average house prices of different types of property by area and county in England and Wales.

www.landregisteronline.gov.uk
Land Register Online provides easy access to details of more than 20 million registered properties in England and Wales. You can download copies of title plans and registers in PDF format for £3 each, payable online by credit card.

www.ros.gov.uk
This is the website of the Registers of Scotland Executive Agency. It provides information about Scotland's land and property. On the website, for a small fee, you can find out about property prices anywhere in Scotland.

www.greenmoves.com
GreenMoves is an advertising website that helps to sell environmentally friendly homes in the United Kingdom and overseas. It is a limited liability company that reinvests its profits in the development

of its website to offer a better service to its customers. In the future it hopes to be able to use some of its profits to offer small grants to help promote the cause of eco-friendly homes.

Further reading

Chiras, D (2002) *The Solar House: Passive heating and cooling*, Chelsea Green, Post Mills, Vermont

Clift, J and Cuthbert, A (2006*) Energy: Use less, save more*, Green Books, Totnes

Clift, J and Cuthbert, A (2006) *Water: Use less, save more*, Green Books, Totnes

Hymers, P (2006) *Converting to an Eco-Friendly Home: The complete handbook*, New Holland, London

4 Home-sellers

Research carried out by the Energy Saving Trust in 2006 showed that 70 per cent of British people believe that energy efficiency is important when buying a new home. Of these, 45 per cent were willing to pay up to £10,000 more for an environmentally friendly home. A survey by the Commission for Architecture and Built Environment found that, in 2004, 87 per cent of UK home-buyers want more information about a property's green credentials and 84 per cent are willing to spend up to 2 per cent more for an eco-friendly home. These figures illustrate that, if you are prepared to make a few changes before selling your home, you should be able to increase your profit margin considerably while also helping the environment.

This chapter provides advice on knowing and understanding what buyers are looking for, making affordable green changes, adding value through environmentally friendly changes, producing a home information pack, presenting your property for sale, marketing your green property to environmentally aware buyers and knowing about relevant grants.

Knowing what buyers are looking for

Environmental awareness is high on the political and public agenda at this present time and is set to gain pace in the future, especially as issues of climate change become more pressing and urgent. The UK government is considering further development of policy to encourage more of us to cut carbon emissions and help to change our lifestyles to reduce the harm on the environment. Many of these changes will involve alterations to our properties and our energy usage. For many people, buying a more energy-efficient home will be a high priority, especially if they are unwilling or unable to make changes to either their existing property or to a property that they are intending to buy. These changes in public and political attitude will be advantageous for people who wish to sell an environmentally friendly home.

To know what buyers are looking for you need to conduct careful research, both into present beliefs and attitudes and into prospective changes in UK policy. Think about your intended market as this will help you to make decisions about appropriate green changes, décor, fixtures, fittings, furnishings, landscaping, gardening and 'dressing' your property. You will find it easier to make a sale if your property is furnished and presented in a way that meets the green expectations of your intended market. Speak to local estate agents to find out what properties are on the market and to arrange a viewing. Visit show homes on new developments and take note of their green credentials and how the property is presented to the target audience. This will help you to think about your market and presenting your property in the most appropriate way.

Monitor local and national government activity – press releases, policy changes, campaigns and media interviews. Important information can be gathered from your local newspapers, radio and television stations, from your local planning authority and from the Department for Communities and Local Government (DCLG) (see Chapter 3). Get to know what is happening in your area and understand how this will affect the local housing market and prospects for selling environmentally friendly homes. Through careful and systematic research you will soon come to understand what buyers are looking for, and how to present your property in the most appropriate manner to reach your target audience.

Making affordable green changes

Once you have identified your target audience you can think about the type of green changes that will appeal to them, and start to make affordable changes to your property. However, you must weigh up the financial pros and cons of each change. Obviously some alterations are much more expensive than others, and you should work out whether it is financially viable and sensible to make them. You also need to think about the amount of work and expertise required to make the changes, and again, make careful decisions about whether the alterations are practical and viable. Table 4.1 gives a summary of the green changes that you could make to your property, including the costs involved and comments about the practicality and viability of undertaking the work.

Table 4.1 Green changes, costs and comments

Green change	Costs	Comments
Convert to a green tariff	Free	Good selling point – saves the potential purchaser having to make the switch.
Install low-energy light bulbs and include in the sale	£4–10	Very easy and cheap to install – good discussion point when showing people around. Choose a type that matches your décor and suits your intended market.
Install draft-proofing on doors and windows	£5–50	How much you pay depends on the type of product that you use. Alterations are cheap and easy to make and can be pointed out in the sales information.
Fit a hot water cylinder jacket and insulate pipes, if appropriate	£15–50	The price depends on product – choose good quality materials, but shop around for the best price. Inform potential purchasers that pipes and cylinders are insulted.
Insulate and draft-proof floors	£10–150	Price depends on type of material and product. More insulation will be needed in older properties with exposed floorboards.
Decorate using environmentally friendly paints and wall coverings	£50–800	Some of these products may be more expensive but you will be able to offset this expense by adding a little to your sale price (see below).
Install new heating controls	£100–1,000	Price depends on the controls that are required. Will need to use a registered professional. All new controls should be discussed and demonstrated.
Install loft insulation	£150–400	Grants are available – use environmentally friendly materials and keep all guarantees to pass on to the new owner. Easy to install yourself.

Table 4.1 Green changes, costs and comments (*continued*)

Green change	Costs	Comments
Install cavity wall insulation	£200–500	Use a professional, but grants are available. Ask for environmentally friendly materials and keep all guarantees to pass on to the new owner. May need to repaint exterior walls which will add to cost.
Install water-saving bathroom suite	£300–2,000	Includes dual flush toilet. Buy a white suite – this doesn't go out of fashion and a new white suite gives the impression of cleanliness and hygiene.
Refurbish using local, recycled and natural materials from sustainable sources	£300–5,000	Price depends on amount of work and materials needed. Keep records of all sources and materials to discuss with potential green purchasers.
Install internal or external wall insulation	£500–5,000	May need to make sure that this does not have a negative influence on the visual impact of your house that could put off potential purchasers.
Fit a high energy-efficiency condensing boiler	£800–3,000	Grants may be available. You will need to use a registered professional to install the boiler and you may need to redecorate and box in pipes to improve the visual impact for viewing.
Install double or triple glazing	£1,500–8,000	Price depends on type of glazing, frames, hinges, locks, and number of windows. Price should include 'making good' around the frame, but check that this is the case. Keep the guarantee to pass on to the new owner. Wooden frames are preferable for eco-homes.

Table 4.1   Green changes, costs and comments (*continued*)

Green change	Costs	Comments
Install solar panels	£3,500–40,000	Grants are available. Keep all guarantees and manuals to pass on to new owners. Will need to use a fully qualified installer and check that conditions are right.
Install wind turbine	£1,500–18,000	Grants are available. Keep all guarantees and manuals to pass on to new owners. Can install yourself if you have the technical ability. Need to check that conditions are right.
Install mini-hydro system	£4,000–25,000	Grants are available. Need right conditions. Will need to use a professional if you don't have the expertise. Keep all guarantees and manuals and be prepared to demonstrate equipment.
Install geo-thermal system	£6,000–18,000	Grants are available. Need right conditions and will need to install early so that you can landscape and allow plants to grow to reduce negative visual impact. Keep all guarantees and manuals.

There are other changes that you may be thinking about, such as installing a rainwater harvesting system or a composting toilet. However, recycling systems such as these tend to appeal only to people who consider themselves to be very eco-friendly, and these types of people are unlikely to pay a high price for a house. Instead, they are more likely to buy a cheap house or land and create their own, personal eco-friendly way of life. Therefore, if you are hoping to make a profit on your eco-changes, you need to appeal to the mainstream green purchaser, rather than those at the more extreme end of the eco-continuum that was discussed in Chapter 1.

Adding value through environmentally friendly changes

If you decide to make environmentally friendly changes to your home it is possible to add value to your house when you decide to sell. Thirty-three potential house buyers who defined themselves as 'environmentally aware' were asked to provide an estimate of how much extra they would be willing to pay for green features in a potential property, and their answers are given in Table 4.2. Although this is only a small sample of potential buyers, the answers give an indication of how much you could add to your selling price through making green changes. However, as with all marketing strategies, you may need to review your price if you fail to make a sale after a certain period, or think about advertising and 'dressing' your property in a more appropriate way (see below).

The figures in Table 4.2 provide an estimate of how much you may be able to add to the value of your house if you make these changes. They suggest that some of the more expensive changes may lead to financial loss rather than profit and should be approached with caution. Also, values depend on the location of your property, the type and number of potential purchasers, fluctuations in the property market and the personal tastes, attitudes and beliefs of potential buyers. You will need to conduct careful research to make sure that you value your house at the right price (see below) and that you only make profitable changes.

Producing a home information pack

From June 2007 the law requires anyone selling a home in England or Wales to put together a home information pack for potential home buyers. A similar scheme may be introduced in Scotland at a later date. These packs are required for most residential property sales of homes marketed for owner occupation. The packs will need to include the following information:

■ An index that lists what is in the pack.

■ A sale statement that summarizes the terms and conditions of the sale.

■ Evidence of title.

Table 4.2 The potential added value of green changes

Green change	Potential added value
Green tariff	Negligible, although a good selling point
Low-energy light bulbs	£8– 31
Draft-proofing on doors and windows	£25–50
Cylinder and pipe insulation	£30–75
Floor insulation	£50–80
Environmentally friendly paint/ materials	£25–100
Loft insulation	£92–220
Heating controls/timers/thermostats	£80–399
Cavity wall insulation	£100–550
Water-saving white bathroom suite	£300–900
Local, recycled and sustainable materials	£300–1,000
Internal or external wall insulation	£300–4,000 (depending on type)
High energy-efficiency condensing boiler	£550–1,500
Double or triple glazing	£1,000–3,000
Solar panels	£2,000–4,000
Wind turbine	£2,000–4,000
Mini-hydro system	£3,000–5,000
Geo-thermal system	£3,000–6,000

■ The results of standard searches, such as local authority enquiries and a drainage and water search.

■ An energy performance certificate (see below).

■ Evidence of ownership – this will depend on the type. Commonhold properties will require a copy of the commonhold community statement; leasehold properties will require a copy of the lease, information on insurance and service charges.

■ A new homes warranty, if appropriate.

■ A home condition report (HCR) (at seller's discretion – this was dropped as a mandatory part of the pack after pressure groups lobbied the government, but the HRC may still become compulsory at a later date).

■ Planning consents (at seller's discretion).

■ Building control certificates (at seller's discretion).

■ Relevant warranties and guarantees (at seller's discretion).

■ Other searches (at seller's discretion).

If you are hoping to market your property to green buyers you may choose to include extra relevant material in the pack, such as alternative technology warranties and guarantees, or alternative technology assessments and energy audits. Packs will remain valid while your home is continuously marketed for sale, usually up to a period of six months. After this time, if your house has not been sold, you may need to update some of the information, such as the local authority searches.

At this present time there is some controversy about the cost of the packs. If the HRC is not included it is believed the packs will cost anything from £200–600. If an HRC is included, the pack could cost £800–1,000. If you are thinking about selling your house from 1 June 2007, up-to-date information about the home information pack can be obtained from the Department for Communities and Local Government (details in Chapter 3) and from the official government home information pack website (details below). To find out about organizations producing home information packs, contact the Association of Home Information Pack Providers (details in Chapter 3).

It is intended that e-conveyancing will be introduced in 2007 and that this should make the conveyancing process easier for all concerned. To save paper and make the process easier it is anticipated that home information packs will be stored electronically so that all the conveyancing information for a property is available easily and quickly (see Chapter 3).

The energy performance certificate

The purpose of the energy performance certificate is to help home-buyers, sellers, landlords and tenants recognize, understand and improve the energy efficiency of buildings. Each building will be issued with a certificate that must be made available when the building is constructed, let or sold. This certificate is a requirement of the EU Performance of Buildings Directive and will be incorporated into home information packs. Landlords will need to make the certificate available to each new tenant when they let their property and certificates will have to be displayed in large public buildings.

The certificate will give each building a SAP rating, and this will equate to an energy rating from A to G, similar to that used on white goods (see Chapter 7). A SAP rating is based on the government's standard assessment procedure for energy rating of dwellings, and is used to demonstrate that buildings comply with the regulations concerning energy efficiency. For more information about SAP ratings consult www.sapratings.com.

The reports will be prepared by a qualified home inspector and will advise consumers on which energy measures might improve the efficiency of their home, from thicker loft insulation and draught-proofing right through to the installation of solar panels. These reports will help purchasers understand the potential of their new property for energy-efficient improvements. More information about the energy performance certificate can be obtained from the DCLG website (details in Chapter 3).

Presenting your green property for sale

There are many things that you can do to increase the chances of selling your green property:

■ Emphasize the green credentials of your property. Make sure that energy-saving fixtures and fittings are included in the sale, and point these out to potential purchasers. If you have carried out your green alterations effectively, your energy performance certificate should help to persuade potential buyers of the greenness of your property.

■ Think about your market and its requirements before people come to view, and familiarize yourself with these. Point out the green features that would appeal to that specific market.

■ Keep all information about the sources of your products and materials. Most green buyers will be very interested to know that the house has been refurbished using environmentally friendly products and materials.

■ Make sure the property is thoroughly clean, including windows. A clean house gives the impression that is has been well cared for, is easy to look after and will provide a healthy, pleasant environment in which to live. Clean, white bathroom suites with water-saving technology can be very appealing.

■ Clean all upholstery and carpets using fragrance-free, environmentally friendly cleaning products. Green viewers will not want to smell artificial air fresheners. Ventilate the property naturally.

■ First impressions are important – make sure that the green credentials of your property are emphasized, and that there is not a negative visual impact for potential buyers. Walk towards your property in the same way as a potential buyer and think about what you see. Make sure everything is neat and tidy, and replace anything that spoils this first impression.

■ 'Dress' your property in a way that will appeal to green purchasers. Follow natural colour schemes and introduce a variety of house plants and furnishings made from natural products. Remove clutter and any items of your property that oppose the green image you are trying to create.

■ Organize rooms and show that each room has a specific purpose that will appeal to green purchasers. Strategically placed items, such as eco-books, wildlife posters and fair-trade items, can help to emphasize your green credentials.

■ Lighting is very important, so use the right type of low-energy light bulb for the room and conditions to create the right mood. Maximize natural daylight if possible – remove fussy window dressings and net curtains. In the evening or on darker days, use lamps and soft lighting to create a warm and homely feel.

■ Point out the savings that are to be made per year on your environmentally friendly source of energy, whether this is an energy-saving boiler or your own source of alternative energy. Make sure the temperature is right when showing people your property – cool in the summer, warm in the winter.

■ Green purchasers tend to be very interested in gardens. Think ahead and grow a variety of food plants if you have the time, as this will appeal to buyers who are thinking of growing their own food. Try to sell your house at a time of year when the garden looks at its best and you can show off your food crop. Find out about your soil type and research the types of plants that flourish in these conditions. Potential purchasers will be happy to discuss this, and it will show that you are knowledgeable and have tended your garden well.

Marketing your green property

When you market your property you need to make decisions about how much you are going to charge, how and where you are going to advertise and who your potential customers might be. Setting the right price is part of your marketing strategy, and needs careful planning and research. Speak to local estate agents and monitor the local housing press to obtain an idea about house prices in the area. The green credentials of your property should enable you to charge a higher price than that charged on other properties, but you must make sure that this is a price that environmentally aware potential purchasers are willing to pay (see above). If you find that your property is not selling, you need to speak to potential customers to find out why they did not make an offer. Listen to what they say and alter your marketing strategy accordingly.

You can advertise your property in four main ways – through an estate agent, on the internet, in the local newspaper or through your local and/or national environmental group newsletter. Using an estate agent to sell your home can reduce the amount of time and effort you would put into advertising yourself, but you should check all contracts carefully and make sure that the estate agent advertises your property effectively and makes every effort to clinch a sale. You will also need to make sure that the agent understands and emphasizes the green credentials of your property.

When choosing an estate agent, make sure the firm is registered with the National Association of Estate Agents or the Ombudsman for Estate Agents (details below). An estate agent by law must give you written confirmation of the instructions to act in the selling of your property on your behalf. The firm must also give you written details of its fees, expenses and business terms before you make an agreement with it.

If you intend to sell privately you will need to produce details of your property. This information will need to be clear, concise, well worded, persuasive, descriptive and effective. Produce a short summary of your property that includes the initial information people want, such as green credentials, location, size and type of house, number of rooms, garden and parking facilities. Then you will need to produce a longer description of the property – more details about the green credentials, facilities in each room (sockets, telephone points), size of each room, number of windows and so on. Be honest and persuasive, avoiding clichés and estate agent jargon, and don't provide misleading or wrong information as this is against the law.

There are a variety of websites offering to sell your property. A well-designed and well-managed site should be listed on all major search engines and in a variety of directories. Some also pay for banner advertisements and link to a variety of related websites. This will ensure that the website receives as many visitors as possible, all of whom have the potential to view your property details. GreenMoves is a useful website for people interested in advertising energy-efficient homes (see Chapter 3). Coolcaves provides an ethical property selling service for people who wish to sell their house online (details below).

When advertising through a property website, find out how much you need to pay, checking whether there is a one-off fee, commission and/or final charges when your property is sold. Also, find out for how long it will advertise your property – it is best to find a place that will advertise until sold. It is also useful to find a website that will allow you to display a photograph of your property, list the green credentials and edit your details when required.

If you are a member of a local and/or national environmental group that has a regular newsletter, it may be possible to place an advert for your house in the small ads section, even if it doesn't usually advertise property for sale. This is a useful way to reach other people who have similar views about environmentally friendly ways of living.

Knowing about grants

Through the Low Carbon Buildings Programme and the Scottish Community and Householder Renewables Initiative, individual householders can apply for grants to help with the installation of renewable sources of energy for their homes (see Appendix 1). To qualify for a grant you must own the property where the renewable energy system is to be installed, you must obtain a quotation from an accredited installer and you must use an approved installer of an approved system.

Other schemes may be available for home owners who are in receipt of certain benefits. These include Warm Front (England), the Home Energy Efficiency Scheme (Wales), Warm Deal (Scotland), Central Heating Programme (Scotland) and Warm Homes (Northern Ireland). However, for some of these schemes you will need to remain in the property for a specified time after the alterations have been made, so you should check on these rules before applying if you are thinking about selling your home. More information about these schemes is available in Appendix 1.

Summary

Making green changes prior to selling can increase the value of your property. However, it is important to conduct careful research into your intended market and make sure that your asking price is realistic. This involves systematic monitoring of the local and national property market, speaking to local estate agents, viewing other properties and making the most of the green credentials of your property. Also, you need to make sure that eco-changes you make to your property are financially viable and will attract potential buyers.

Once you have successfully sold your green property and purchased a new house, you can think about obtaining a mortgage that fits well with your green philosophy. These issues are discussed in the next chapter.

Useful organizations

NAEA is the largest professional estate agency organization in the United Kingdom. All members must operate to a professional code of practice and rules of conduct. A list of members is available on the website.

National Association of Estate Agents
Arbon House, 21 Jury Street
Warwick CV34 4EH
Tel: 01926 496 800
Fax: 01926 400 953
E-mail: info@naea.co.uk
Website: www.naea.co.uk

The Ombudsman for Estate Agents (OEA)

OEA has been established to provide a free, fair and independent service to buyers and sellers of residential property in the United Kingdom. You can find contact details of members in your area from the website, access housing survey information and find out about their code of practice.

Ombudsman for Estate Agents
Beckett House, 4 Bridge Street
Salisbury
Wilts SP1 2LX
Tel: 01722 333 306
Fax: 01722 332 296
E-mail: admin@oea.co.uk
Website: www.oea.co.uk

Useful websites

www.coolcaves.com
This website provides a property selling service for people who wish to sell their house online. It belongs to an ethical property company that donates 20 per cent of your fee to Centrepoint, the youth homelessness charity. When you advertise your property you pay a one-off fee of £95 (2006/07 prices) and then your property is advertised on a large network of property websites.

www.homeinformationpacks.gov.uk
This is the government website that describes the home information packs in detail for industry and members of the public. On this website you can find up-to-date information leading up to the launch of the packs.

Further reading

The Home Information Pack Regulations 2006: Procedural guidelines, available from the DCLG or to download from its website (details in Chapter 3)
Personal Searches: Guidance for local authorities and personal searchers, available from the DCLG or to download from its website (details in Chapter 3)

5 Borrowers

Most of us who are thinking about buying a property, either as homeowners or as investors, will have to borrow money to do so. If this is the case it is important to know that the lender understands and works within your green philosophy.

To choose an appropriate lender, therefore, you need to define your borrowing philosophy so that you are clear about the type of lender and the type of mortgage that will be suitable for your needs, and suitable for the property that you wish to purchase or remortgage. This chapter offers advice about these issues along with information about ethical borrowing, mortgages for environmentally sensitive new build and renovation, researching green lenders and using ethical financial advisers.

Defining your borrowing philosophy

When choosing a mortgage and a lender you need to think about the environmental and ethical issues that are important to you, and match these with your financial and personal circumstances. You also need to be realistic about your chances of getting a mortgage – some ethical lending companies have very strict criteria and all will need detailed evidence to show that you are able to repay the loan. Your green philosophy discussed in Chapter 1 will provide a useful starting point, as it will help you to think about your ethical and environmental principles. However, where mortgages are concerned, there are other issues you need to consider when defining your borrowing philosophy and thinking about financial constraints. These include the following points:

■ Is it important that you choose a lender that operates to strict environmental and ethical criteria? If this is the case you will need to find out whether the company will lend money for your

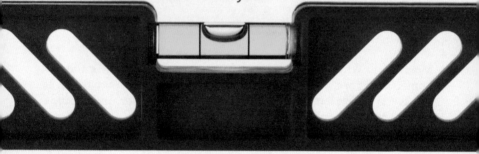

Financing your self-build project

Switch on the TV or browse the shelves in your local newsagents and there seems to be an increasing number of programmes and magazines concerned with self-build. More and more people are seriously researching the option of building their own home. Finding the plot, working with an architect who can design your vision and getting a builder to help realise that dream are all part of the challenge, but there can be a danger that you get so engrossed in these things that you don't spend enough time on what some may call the more mundane element – sorting the finances for the project.

However, having the wrong lender could cause just as many problems as working with the wrong builder! Just think back to those TV programmes and the case studies in the magazines – budgets and finance are too often the cause of tension and problems. At Leeds Building Society, we aim to make the money side of things as straightforward and smooth as possible – letting you concentrate on the exciting parts!

A self-build project is a way for you to realise your dream and not have to make compromises. At Leeds Building Society, we've developed our Self-Build offering to reduce the compromises you have to make. We take a tailored and flexible approach to our lending – for example, releasing the funds at appropriate stages throughout the project, with the flexibility to vary these staged releases. Also, unlike many other lenders, the majority of our product range is available to self-builders – whether you want a fixed rate, variable, tracker or discount mortgage – meaning you can be sure you have access to some of our most competitive mortgage rates and don't have to be tied to a so called 'specialist' self-build mortgage. We can also help you with funding for the initial purchase of the plot – up to 85% of the current value – as long as outline planning permission, building regs and a cost schedule are provided.

Whilst a self-build project can be immensely rewarding, it can be stressful, but you will find the staff in our 70 branches across the UK and UK-based call centre, all very friendly, helpful and professional. They will take the time to explain all of the options to help you decide on the mortgage that best suits your needs. We regularly undertake research and over 90% of our customers tell us they are satisfied with the service we provide. This service has been recognised by others too – we were Mortgage Magazine's Best Building Society for 2006 and received a Gold award from Lending Excellence magazine.

With increasing numbers of people wanting to build sustainably and limit their impact on the community, you can be sure that Leeds Building Society is on your side. As a mutual building society, we are owned by our members, not by shareholders, so you can be sure we have our members' interest at heart. We are 100% committed to remaining mutual and always aim to work with the people in the communities in which we operate.

We have already helped many others build the home of their dreams and you can be sure – when you take that exciting first step on the road to building your dream – that we'll be fully committed to helping you.

Leeds
Building Society

proposed project. These lenders tend to have strict criteria about the type of project or property on which they will lend, and unless your property is able to meet these criteria, you are unlikely to be successful in your application.

▪ Are you interested in a lender that uses ethical principles to guide its own activities, such as how it invests money and how it treats its employees?

▪ Is it important that the lender provides money for properties that meet certain standards in terms of eco-friendliness? Can you be sure that your property will meet these standards? What are the financial and other penalties if you fail to meet these standards?

▪ Do you want the lender you use to be owned by its members rather than shareholders, such as a mutual building society?

▪ Are you happy to receive a loan from any company, as long as it can assure you it invests in ethical funds?

▪ How much can you afford to borrow? Can you afford to lose money or take a loss if the housing market slumps, and can you weather fluctuations in the market? Will the green credentials of your property help it to sell if the housing market slumps and you need to make a quick sale?

▪ Can you continue with the mortgage payments if you are prevented from working/earning as a result of illness?

▪ What protection is offered with the mortgage? Do you need to look at other types of insurance? What insurance will be offered on ethical or environmental mortgages, and will it be adequate for your needs? Does the insurance company have a code of ethical practice? All borrowers will need to arrange life assurance and think about mortgage protection cover. If you intend to let your property you need to think about buy-to-let insurance or rent guarantee insurance, as these will cover you if you have problems letting your property. Some lenders also recommend that you take out critical illness cover or accident, sickness and unemployment insurance. More information about various types of ethical insurance can be obtained from the EIRIS and EIG websites (details below and in Chapter 6). For contact details of ethical insurance companies, consult the EIRIS factsheet 'Ethical mortgages and insurance' (details below).

When choosing a lender or an insurance company you may need to think about disregarding companies that are involved in activities with which you disagree, such as the arms trade, pornography or gambling, and consider only those companies that take part in activities and investment with which you agree. This is called positive and negative screening, and is discussed in more depth in Chapter 6.

Knowing about ethical mortgages

There are various ways that you could obtain a mortgage that can be considered to be ethical. The first is to use an organization that has a strict ethical code of practice to guide its investment. For example, in 1992 the Co-operative Bank decided to introduce ethical standards that would govern the type of organizations to which the bank would and would not offer business. These standards are based on the concerns of its customers, and include issues such as human rights, the arms trade, global trade, genetic modification, ecological impact and animal welfare. If you decide to take out a mortgage with the Co-operative Bank, for every year that your mortgage exists, it will make a payment to Climate Care, an organization dedicated to combating global warming. Projects it has supported over the years include planting new forests in Uganda, helping locals to build fuel-efficient stoves in Madagascar, and helping locals to build 'bio-gas' household systems in India. More information about the Co-operative ethical policy and range of mortgages can be obtained from its website (www.co-operativebank.co.uk).

The second way to obtain an ethical mortgage is to look at green options that are offered by more mainstream lenders. For example, the Norwich and Peterborough Building Society offers a 'green mortgage' on new homes that have a SAP rating of 100 or higher or on an existing property that you want to make more energy efficient. For every green mortgage that is taken out 40 trees are planted, eight each year for the first five years, by the CarbonNeutral Company. This is a company that works with its partners to plant and maintain forests and offset the damage done to the environment by businesses and individuals. More information about the Norwich and Peterborough Building Society green mortgage can be obtained from its website (www.npbs.co.uk), and more information about the CarbonNeutral Company can be obtained from its website (www.carbonneutral.com).

The third way to obtain an ethical mortgage is to approach a company that will only invest in property that gives an 'ecological payback', such as the Ecology Building Society (details below). Mortgages will be offered on properties to improve energy efficiency, for ecological renovation, to improve and make habitable derelict and dilapidated properties and for small-scale ecological enterprises. It is even possible through this company for individuals, groups and charities to obtain a mortgage to purchase woodland, meadows, fields or houseboat moorings.

The Ecology Building Society has developed the 'C-Change' mortgage discount as an incentive to residential owner-occupiers who wish to make changes to increase the energy efficiency of their home. The incentive offers a 1 per cent discount on its standard variable rate on funds borrowed to install energy-efficient measures or renewable energy sources, and the discount is guaranteed for the remainder of the mortgage term. This includes changes such as installing roof, floor and wall insulation, fitting double or triple glazing, installing low water-use appliances and a condensing boiler. It also includes the installation of renewable energy sources such as solar water heating, photovoltaics, wind turbines, ground source heat pumps or biomass heating (see Chapter 2).

Another way to obtain an ethical mortgage is to use a mutual building society that is owned by members rather than shareholders. Some of these building societies are developing their own codes of ethics, guided by the concerns of their customers. These principles are now having more of an influence on investment and lending decisions within these organizations. Contact the building society in which you are interested for more information, or consult an ethical financial adviser who will be able to offer advice about suitable organizations (see below).

If you decide to take out an interest-only mortgage the lender will need to be satisfied that you have taken out a suitable policy that will enable you to repay the loan at the end of the term. To do this you can take out an endowment, ISA or pension policy. Through these types of funds it is possible to use fund managers that will only invest in ethical funds, where investment decisions are influenced by social, environmental and/or ethical criteria (see Chapter 6). Therefore, another option open to you is to take out the best deal interest-only mortgage you can find and then invest your money through ethical funds. However, investment decisions of this nature should be taken carefully as the money you get back on your investment may not match the sum you borrowed at the end of the term.

The choice of ethical mortgages and ethical investment opportunities is increasing annually. You should seek impartial advice or conduct careful research into the type of mortgage that best suits your needs and enables you to obtain the best deal. As a useful starting point, consult the EIRIS factsheet 'Ethical mortgages and insurance', available as a PDF on its website (details below).

Mortgages for green new build and renovation

In cases of new build or renovation and conversion, most borrowers will need more than the initial purchase amount to complete the property. In these cases some lenders will offer mortgages on property under construction. The loan is paid out in stages so that the loan to value ratio does not rise too high at any point. This is a percentage figure of the loan amount in relation to the property value. It is possible to receive 85–95 per cent of the final value of the property, or 85–95 per cent of the total costs of the project, which includes purchase of the land or property. Some lenders may specify that the renovation or build reaches certain stages before extra money is released, whereas others will release further sums based on the increasing value of the property as work continues. Some lenders will specify that the project is completed within a set period of time.

If you intend to apply for a mortgage on a new build, renovation or conversion project you will need to supply the lender with details of the following:

- outline or full planning permission that has been granted;
- plans for the work you wish to undertake;
- a project timescale;
- a full breakdown of costs including builders' quotations or your own estimates;
- a deposit;
- evidence of sufficient working capital;
- evidence that you can repay the mortgage.

If you are intending to renovate or convert a building to let to tenants, it is possible to obtain a buy-to-let mortgage from some companies that specialize in ethical mortgages. Although lending criteria vary between companies, in general you will need to be a homeowner with a clean borrowing history, and you will need to have been registered on the electoral register for over three years. Some companies place a limit on the number of properties that you can borrow against and make available for letting.

For buy-to-let mortgages the amount that you can borrow is based on the anticipated rental income that will be generated by the property, and in most cases, this will need to be 30–35 per cent more than the monthly mortgage payment. The amount that companies will lend varies, but is usually in the region of 75–85 per cent of the purchase price or valuation, whichever is lower. Further funds may be available as the renovation or build work continues and the price of the property increases. Again, the amount of funds available will be within a specified percentage of the total valuation of the property. All lenders will want to know that you have sufficient funds to pay a deposit and carry out the required work. In large projects some lenders will insist that they appoint an architect to supervise the work and issue a certificate upon satisfactory completion. Most will insist that the property is let on individual assured shorthold tenancies (short assured tenancies in Scotland) for periods not exceeding 12 months at a time, although responsibility for letting the property remains with you as the landlord.

Researching and choosing green lenders

Once you have decided that you would like an ethical mortgage and/ or a suitable mortgage for environmentally friendly improvements, you need to think about your green borrowing philosophy and make sure that any lender you choose agrees with and understands your philosophy. Perhaps one of the easiest ways to do this is to use an ethical financial adviser, as these people know what products are available on the market and will be able to match your green philosophy with these companies and their products. However, other people prefer to conduct their own research. Whether you choose to use an adviser or make your own choices, it is important to make sure that you are clear about what you are looking for, and how your criteria match your current and future personal and financial circumstances. The following tips will help you to do this:

▊ Define your green borrowing philosophy and make sure that others are able to understand what is important to you.

▊ Identify and prioritize your short-term and long-term financial and environmental goals.

■ Check your existing resources and think about how you would like these to improve in the future.

■ Seek appropriate, impartial advice from experts. For example, you might find it useful to discuss your plans with your accountant, your architect or your project manager. Experienced professionals will have ideas or contacts within the industry that may be able to suggest suitable lenders.

■ Ask to see the ethical codes of all potential lenders.

■ Use positive and negative screening methods to choose a suitable lender (see Chapter 6).

■ Shop around for the best deal and choose products/investors suitable for your needs. Don't accept the first offer of cash – keep your options open.

■ Don't rush into a decision. Discuss options with your family and/or business partners.

■ Once you think you have found a suitable organization, check that it is authorized by the Financial Services Authority (FSA), by using the Firm Check Service on the FSA website (details below) or by contacting the Consumer Contact Centre on 0845 606 1234.

■ Never sign anything you don't understand. Don't be bullied or persuaded into make decisions that are not right, and don't be afraid to say no if something doesn't seem quite suitable. If you are unsure of anything, you can always seek a second opinion.

■ Review your financial situation and green borrowing philosophy on a regular basis. Make sure that lenders and investment funds don't change their criteria in a way that does not suit your green philosophy. Taking out a mortgage can be a long-term process, and you need to make sure that your principles are not compromised over the course of the term.

If you decide to find your own mortgage or other financial products without seeking advice, you must realize that the individuals or companies that you approach are trying to sell you their products and may not have your best interests at heart. However, many organizations that follow ethical guidelines believe that it is important not to oversell their products, overstretch their customers or offer products that are unsuitable. When you carry out your research you should try to gauge whether this is the case with the company in which you are interested. If you cannot be sure that an organization is offering products that are suitable, you should think about seeking independent financial advice. Today there are a number of financial advisers that specialize in offering advice about ethical products and companies.

Using ethical financial advisers

There are three types of financial adviser:

■ Independent financial advisers (IFAs) provide advice tailored to your needs. They will have a large number of products from which to choose, and make sure that the most appropriate choices are made on your behalf.

■ Multi-tied advisers can only sell products from a limited number of companies to which they are tied. However, within this range they will try to recommend the most appropriate products for your needs.

■ Tied advisers can only sell products from the one company to which they are tied, and are usually employed by that company. Within the limited range of products they will try to find the best one for you.

If you wish to find out about a large range of ethical products you should use an independent financial adviser. However, if you have already conducted thorough research and you know the type of products that would suit your needs you can seek further advice from a tied or multi-tied adviser. When you first meet a financial adviser it may be unclear which type he or she is, so make sure that you ask, as advisers are obliged to supply this information.

Only firms and their agents authorized by the FSA are allowed to give advice about mortgages, and they must follow certain rules when doing so. This includes giving you a document that details the service they can provide, including the mortgages they offer, and details about whether there is either an up-front fee payable or commission on mortgages they recommend. They must also give you a key facts document that summarizes the important features of the mortgage recommended. This could include issues of ethical investment and/or the lender's code of ethical practice if you have indicated that this is important to you. Once you have received advice you will then be given a personalized illustration of key facts about the mortgage.

You can use the EIRIS Financial Adviser Directory to find an ethical financial adviser in your area (details below). The directory can be searched by postcode or by using the alphabetical listing. Alternatively, you can use the Ethical Investors Group to obtain advice about ethical mortgages (see Chapter 6). This organization has been set up to provide specialist financial advice to people who are interested in ethical and environmental issues. Through the ethical mortgage department you can receive advice about all borrowing-related issues, types of mortgage, life assurance, investment options, and discuss your ethical and environmental philosophy, which will be taken into account when products are recommended.

The Personal Finance Society (PFS) is the professional body for financial advisers and people in related roles (details below). It was created in 2005 after the merger of the Life Insurance Association and the Society of Financial Advisers. The PFS helps members to become better qualified and provides a useful directory for people wishing to find a financial adviser or chartered financial planner. You can search the database for a financial adviser by type of product, gender, payment procedure and postcode.

Summary

When buying or investing in property most of us need to borrow money, but this does not mean that we have to compromise our ethical principals or lose out financially. Today there are a number of lenders willing to provide a mortgage on eco-properties, either new build or renovation, and there are a variety of companies that use ethical principles to guide their investment and working practices.

In addition to borrowing money to buy or build your property, there are other types of property investment in which you may wish to become involved, and again, this type of investment does not mean that you have to compromise your ethical principles or lose out financially. These issues are discussed in the next chapter.

Useful organizations

Ecology Building Society

The Ecology Building Society is a mutual organization that grants mortgages on properties and projects that help the environment, such as renovation of empty or derelict buildings, eco-new build, organic smallholdings, earth shelters and traditional construction buildings. It will lend to owner-occupiers, landlords, housing cooperatives, housing associations, companies and individuals.

Ecology Building Society
7 Belton Road
Silsden, Keighley
West Yorkshire BD20 0EE
Tel: 0845 674 5566
Fax: 01535 650 780
E-mail: info@ecology.co.uk
Website: www.ecology.co.uk

Ethical Investment Research Service (EIRIS)

EIRIS carries out independent research into corporate behaviour. This provides information for people who want to invest ethically, helping them to make informed and responsible investment decisions. IFAs who offer ethical advice about mortgages are listed in the online directory which you can access from the website.

Ethical Investment Research Service
80–84 Bondway
London SW8 1SF
Tel: 020 7840 5700
Fax: 020 7735 5323
E-mail: ethics@eiris.org
Website: www.eiris.org

Useful websites

www.fsa.gov.uk
The FSA is the independent regulator set up by the government to look after the financial services industry and protect customers. The FSA website provides a useful comparative table for mortgages, enabling you to search for, and compare, the types of mortgage that might suit your needs.

www.thepfs.org
The Personal Finance Society (PFS) is the merged professional association of the Life Insurance Association and the Society of Financial Advisers. Visit this website to use the online directory of financial advisers in the United Kingdom. The website contains useful information about various types of investment and obtaining financial advice.

www.unbiased.co.uk
This is the Independent Financial Adviser Promotion (IFAP) website. It is a directory of 9,000 individuals and organizations, covering over 90 per cent of registered IFAs in the United Kingdom. On the website you can search for an IFA in your area by gender, investment type, qualification and the method in which you would like to pay for advice.

www.cml.org.uk
The Council of Mortgage Lenders is the trade association for mortgage lenders in the United Kingdom. It is a major provider of market information, economic analyses and housing statistics. It also produces *Housing Finance Online*, which is a useful online publication featuring topical articles on the housing and mortgage markets. All articles are free to download.

Further reading

EIRIS (2002) *Ethical Mortgages and Insurance*, available as download-able PDF from www.eiris.org. This is a useful publication that discusses a variety of ethical mortgage and insurance products and providers, along with contact details of those listed.

6 Investors

As property owners, all of us make a financial investment. This might be in the property itself, our mortgage, endowments, life assurance, individual savings accounts (ISAs), self-invested personal pensions (SIPPs) and other pensions. Yet many of us have little control, influence or knowledge about how our money is invested on our behalf. Although we can make decisions about our own property that meet our personal values and green philosophy, decisions of this nature can be taken out of our hands where other investments are concerned.

However, this does not have to be the case. It is possible to make investment decisions based on your personal values and ethical principles. Through careful research and investment in funds run by specialist managers it is possible to invest both in progressive companies that share your values and in green property, without affecting the return on your investment.

This chapter offers advice on defining your investment philosophy, finding out about ethical investment opportunities, researching suitable companies and seeking the advice of professionals.

Defining your investment philosophy

When choosing the types of funds, companies and green property in which to invest, you need to think about the ethical issues that are important to you. Your green philosophy discussed in Chapter 1 will provide a useful starting point, as it will help you to think about your ethical principles. However, where investments are concerned, there are other issues you need to consider when defining your investment philosophy. To help you to choose the right investment, think about positive and negative screening.

Positive screening involves making decisions based on positive attributes. It will include the following issues:

■ Is it important to you to choose a company and/or property that help to contribute towards a safe and healthy environment by reducing harmful emissions, saving energy and using environmentally sound building materials?

■ Are you interested in companies that produce or offer ecologically superior products, or ecologically superior premises?

■ Are you interested in companies that use ecological principles to drive their new product design, development or investment?

■ Is it important that you only invest in companies that produce products or take part in activities with which you agree?

■ Is it important that an organization contributes to charitable groups or uses profits for the benefit of members?

■ Do you intend to invest in companies that pay a decent living wage to their employees and provide good working conditions?

Negative screening involves making decisions about funds, companies or property that you would exclude because of their type or because of activities in which they are involved. This negative screening could include some or all of the following:

■ Investment and/or involvement in products or activities with which you disagree: for example, tobacco, gambling, weapons, nuclear energy, animal testing and pornography.

■ Companies that have a poor record of product and/or employee safety.

■ Companies that have problems with employee relations or exploitation of workers.

■ Multinational companies that have a poor record of community/country involvement.

■ Investment and/or involvement in countries that have problems with human rights.

■ Investment and/or involvement with countries that are doing nothing to reduce environmental harm.

■ Companies and/or properties that cause environmental damage.

■ Properties that have little potential for green development (see Chapter 9).

Types of ethical property investment

Ethical investment is also called socially responsible investment (SRI). There are now many different types of SRI that you can select to provide income and/or growth, and there are a variety of different types of green property investment with which you can become directly or indirectly involved.

Property investment

It is possible to invest in commercial and residential projects, in the United Kingdom and overseas, that are both environmentally responsible and financially rewarding. There are two main reasons for this. First, environmental concerns are growing among the public, business and political communities, and second, developers and investors realize the greater potential for saving money and making larger profits over the long term, even though short-term costs may be higher. At the time of writing the green building market is a profitable niche with relatively little competition. In this market, potential customers are willing to pay more for environmentally friendly properties.

There are a variety of ways in which you can invest in green property:

■ Self-build an eco-friendly house for personal use or to let to tenants (see Chapter 10).

■ Refurbish or renovate a property using green materials for personal use, to let to tenants or to let commercially (see Chapter 9).

■ Invest in a buy-to-let green property (see Chapter 7). Property prices are still rising, there will always be a demand for rental properties and there are an increasing number of tenants interested in green issues.

■ Buy shares in an ethical property development company for either commercial or residential property. Use the negative and positive screening methods described above to make sure that the company meets your green criteria, and consult Companies House to check the legitimacy of the company (details below).

▌ Invest in eco-tourism building projects worldwide. Over recent years a number of projects have been set up aimed at conserving land or protecting wildlife in endangered areas. To do this eco-villages have been established for environmentally friendly tourists who are also the investors. Depending on the amount you invest, you have a guaranteed length of stay in the village, either at no cost or at a reduced cost, and if you opt into the rental pool you will receive an income from the property, usually on a monthly basis. As with any investment of this nature, careful research must be conducted to check the viability, reliability and legitimacy of the company.

▌ Invest in overseas eco-development projects. As the demand for environmentally friendly properties increases worldwide, savvy developers are providing the opportunity for people to invest in properties overseas that are built following ecological principles. These include lessening the impact of the development on the local environment, protecting biodiversity and helping the local community by providing training, jobs and a decent wage, without exploitation. Investors have the opportunity to buy properties outright, or hold a stake or percentage of a property. Again, you must conduct careful research to check the viability, reliability and legitimacy of any company in which you choose to invest. You should also consider the stability and economic climate of the country in which the development is situated.

▌ Invest in property through your own property pension fund (see below).

Personal pensions

There are two ways that you can use your pension to invest in property: first, through a property fund run by a specialist fund manager, and second, through self-investment in a specific property.

Property funds

If you are interested in property investment it is possible to invest your money in commercial property, offices, shops, factories and warehouses, but you will need to choose a specialist fund manager that offers this service. Not all pension companies will offer this service and only a few will offer property funds that specialize in green property. Also, because the property market can be unpredictable, most will suggest that you spread your investment into other funds, such as bonds and equity funds, and you will need to make sure that these funds also match your green philosophy. This will help you to receive funds from elsewhere should the property market be in decline when you choose to take your pension. A good ethical financial adviser will be able to offer advice on suitable funds.

In property funds the value of units increases with the rents received from the lease of properties. Holdings are independently valued periodically, and if this reveals an increase in value, the value of the units increases. Your investment performance, therefore, is dependent on the property market and on the skill of your fund manager.

There are two types of pension that will enable you to invest in a property fund. First, *personal pension plans* are available to UK residents under the age of 75. In these schemes money is invested by an approved fund manager and the funds are built up for retirement. Ethical and property fund choices have been available for some time on many personal pensions. More information can be obtained from the Ethical Investment Association (details below).

Second, *stakeholder pension schemes* are available to UK residents under the age of 75, whether or not they are in employment. Unlike most personal pension plans, there are no penalties on stopping contributions to an individual's fund or on transferring the benefits to another scheme. Some stakeholder pension contracts offer ethical and property investment choices. More information can be obtained from an ethical financial adviser in your area. Details of these can be obtained from the Ethical Investment Association (details below).

More information about both these types of pension can be obtained from the Pensions Advisory Group or from the Department for Work and Pensions (DWP) (details below).

Self-investment

Personal pensions can be used to invest in commercial property, and since April 2006 in residential property. Property pension savings offer considerable tax advantages; in the short term for deductions against income or corporation tax for personal contributions, and in the long term on tax-free lump sums upon retirement and lump sums free of inheritance tax payable on death. Also, the pension scheme does not have to pay tax on the rent it receives from the property and there is no capital gains tax to be paid when the property is sold.

In many cases you will be able to raise a mortgage to purchase the property, subject to strict HM Revenue and Customs limits. For some types of pension it is possible to choose your own property and act as manager of the property. This enables you to match the type of property and method of management with your green philosophy. However, you will need a professional to run the pension fund because you need to use an authorized provider to qualify for tax relief.

There are two main options. *Small self-administered schemes (SSAS)* are set up by companies for selected employees, often the company's directors, and tend to be used by family-run and small businesses. They are not applicable if you are self-employed. These schemes can be costly to run, and if you are interested in this type of pension you should seek professional advice to determine whether it is the most appropriate route for you to take. Second, *self-invested personal pensions (SIPPS)* can be set up by employed or self-employed individuals with the help of a professional trustee and an administrator. These people or organizations must be HM Revenue and Customs approved. To buy a property the SIPP must have sufficient funds, either outright or with a mortgage, and it is restricted in the amount that it can borrow. More information about SIPPS can be obtained from the SIPP Provider Group (details below).

When considering property for your pension you must realize that although over the long term property can prove to be a good investment, this may not always be the case. As with any property investment you need to make careful decisions about buying the right property for the right price in the right location. You also need to realize that there may be periods when the property remains untenanted, and that your assets are not liquid – properties can take a long time to sell, which can be a problem if you need cash urgently.

The property you buy can be freehold or leasehold, but you will need to make sure that there is at least 50 years to run on the lease. If you are interested in purchasing an eco-friendly property, good green credentials can add value and make it easier to let to tenants who understand the savings that can be made on energy bills. It is possible to redevelop, refurbish and extend the property using cash that has accumulated in the pension scheme or within the limits of the mortgage, subject to the usual planning permissions and regulations. It is also possible to redevelop the property for onward sale, although if your pension scheme is seen to be 'trading' it could be liable to pay corporation tax.

If you are interested in this type of pension you should seek professional advice, as HM Revenue and Customs has strict rules, regulations and procedures that should be followed. Property pension funds can be set up fairly quickly, and it is possible to transfer certain pension schemes, although care should be taken to make sure that any funds that are transferred receive a fair valuation and that you do not lose any valuable protection under your existing scheme. Comprehensive, user-friendly advice about all types of pension can be obtained from the Pensions Advisory Service (details below). Further information can be obtained from the Department for Work and Pensions website (www.dwp.gov.uk).

Endowments

Today there are a number of ethical fund providers who will provide house purchase endowment products through ethical funds. However, all endowment products contain an element of risk, as has been highlighted by the media over recent years. To avoid problems you should seek professional advice from an advisor who offers advice on ethical investment. Use the member's directory on the Ethical Investment Research Service website to find an adviser in your area (details below).

Individual savings accounts

Individual savings accounts (ISAs) can be linked to interest-only mortgages, with the proceeds from the ISA investment used to pay off the loan at the end of the term. The ISA holds shares, in either individual companies or unit and investment trusts, and the proceeds are allowed to grow tax-free. There are a variety of ethical ISAs currently available, and at time of writing, ethical funds are marginally outperforming their peers over the short term, illustrating that you do not have to compromise financial returns for ethical principals. Some experts believe that this situation will continue, as environmental issues are high on the political agenda, whereas others believe that returns from ethical ISAs have peaked. As with any investment, there are risks attached and you should seek independent financial advice before you make an investment.

Life assurance

There are a number of ethical fund providers that offer life assurance products through their ethical funds. All mortgage companies insist that you have adequate life assurance to cover you and your family in the event of your death, but you don't have to compromise your ethical principles when choosing a life assurance policy. You can find out which ethical funds provide life assurance products by consulting 'Investment funds – the EIRIS ethical fund selector', available on the EIRIS website (see Chapter 5).

Researching and questioning organizations

If you already hold investment funds there are questions that you can ask to find out more about the type of investment that is being made on your behalf. All financial providers make use of the money you have invested when you are not using it, so question them to find out what they are doing with it. They must supply this information when requested. If you find that you are not happy with the investments being made on your behalf you can discuss this with your financial provider to find out if it can, and is willing to, make changes. If it is not able to make changes, you can withdraw your funds and consider investing elsewhere, although you will need to consider financial penalties and fees that may be payable.

When researching new organizations, and questioning your current financial services provider, the following points will help:

■   Ask to see the company's code of business ethics.

■   Ask about the company's environmental and social policies, and how these apply to investing your money.

■   For pensions, ask to see a statement of investment principles, which sets out the principles employed by the company when investing your money. If this does not include environmental and social issues, find out why.

■   Ethical and socially responsible fund managers carry out both positive and negative screening when deciding on investment opportunities. Find out whether such screening is carried out by your financial service provider. If not, find out why not.

■   If you are intending to buy shares, contact the company direct for more information about its ethical policy. Companies with a good ethical record will be happy to supply you with all the information you need.

Using professionals

When choosing a finance professional you need to make sure that you choose an experienced, qualified, independent person who agrees with, or is able to understand, your green philosophy. You should also make sure that you read any documents you are given, including the small print, before signing a contract or entering into an agreement. A good adviser will take time to get to know you, and will ask relevant questions about your investment plans and your green philosophy, if you have indicated to him or her that this is important to you. When choosing a suitable professional, you should consider the following points:

■ Is he or she a member of a professional association? Does this professional association ensure that the professional keeps up to date with his/her training and abides by a code of conduct?

■ Is he or she authorized to offer financial and investment advice? For how long has he/she been authorized? You can check whether a professional is authorized by contacting the FSA Consumer Contact Centre or the FSA Firm Check Service (see Chapter 5).

■ Does he or she have a clear understanding of ethical investment and SRI issues? Is he or she keeping abreast of new issues and changes in the market?

■ Does he or she understand your green philosophy, and is he/she able to incorporate your views into your financial planning and/or investment?

■ Does he or she routinely ask about the ethics of companies he/she recommends for investment?

■ Is he or she willing to recommend previous clients who can act as referees?

■ Is the professional tied to a particular company? If this is the case he or she will not be able to recommend suitable products that are not provided by that company (see Chapter 5).

■ How is the adviser paid, by fees or by commission? If you are to pay a fee, how much will you need to pay? If payment is by commission, does the adviser tend to recommend specific products that attract a higher commission?

❚ Are you able to get on with the professional? Has rapport been established? Do you trust him or her to do the best for you? If not, move on to another professional.

Summary

If you conduct careful research and work with professionals who understand the issues that concern you, it is possible to make investment decisions that match your green philosophy. Ethical investment and SRI are becoming increasingly popular, with more and varied opportunities available. This means that you do not have to compromise your green principles or lose out financially when you make investments.

One of the most popular ways to invest in property in the United Kingdom is to buy a property to let to tenants. This provides an opportunity to work within your green philosophy, advertise the green credentials of your property and to let it to like-minded tenants who will be able to respect your views. These issues are discussed in the next chapter.

Useful organizations

UK Social Investment Forum (UKSIF)

UKSIF was launched in 1991 and is a membership network for UK SRI. Members include retail and institutional fund managers, financial advisers, SRI research providers, consultants, trade unions, banks, building societies, NGOs and interested individuals. A member directory is available on the website along with useful information about SRI.

UK Social Investment Forum
Holywell Centre, 1 Phipp Street
London EC2A 4PS
Tel: 020 7749 9950
E-mail: info@uksif.org
Website: www.uksif.org

Ethical Investors Group

The Ethical Investors Group has been established to provide a specialist financial advice service to people who care about the world and its preservation. Advice is offered to individuals, charities, not-for-profit groups and commercial organizations. Fifty per cent of the profit earned from commission and fees is distributed to charities and groups nominated by clients. Contact the group for information about its fees. On its website you can use the Ethical Fund Directory, which is a comprehensive list of all ethical funds available in the UK.

Ethical Investors Group
Montpellier House, 47 Rodney Road
Cheltenham GL50 1HX
Tel: 01242 539 848
Fax: 01242 539 851
E-mail: info@ethicalinvestors.co.uk
Website: www.ethicalinvestors.co.uk

Companies House

The main functions of Companies House are to incorporate and dissolve limited companies, examine and store company information delivered under the Companies Act and make this information available to the public.

Companies House
Crown Way
Maindy, Cardiff CF14 3UZ
Tel: 0870 33 33 636
E-mail: enquiries@companies-house.gov.uk
Website: www.companieshouse.gov.uk

The Pensions Advisory Service (TPAS)

TPAS is an independent, voluntary organization that is grant-aided by the Department for Work and Pensions. TPAS offers useful and down-to-earth information about pensions, helping to explain complex rules and regulations in a way that can be understood by the layperson. It will also help members of the public who have a problem, complaint or dispute with their occupational or private pension arrangements.

The Pensions Advisory Service
11 Belgrave Road
London SW1V 1RB
Tel: 0845 6012 823
Fax: 020 7233 8016
E-mail: enquiries@pensionsadvisoryservice.org.uk
Website: www.pensionsadvisoryservice.org.uk

Useful websites

www.ethicalinvestment.org.uk
This is the website of the Ethical Investors Association (EIA), which is an association of financial advisers from around the United Kingdom who promote ethical investment and SRI. The aim of the organization is to increase public access to financial advice on ethical investment and SRI, and raise standards among financial advisers offering this type of advice. On the website you can obtain advice about ethical investment and access a database of ethical financial advisers in the United Kingdom.

www.sipp-provider-group.org.uk
The SIPP Provider Group is the representative body for SIPP operators in negotiations and consultation with HM Revenue and Customs, the Department of Work and Pensions and other government bodies. It does not offer advice to the public, but on the website you can find more information about SIPPS and a directory of members.

Further reading

Hancock, J (2005) *An Investor's Guide to Ethical and Socially Responsible Investment Funds: A unique analysis of UK based investment funds*, Kogan Page, London

7 Landlords

Landlords sometimes have a reputation for being unscrupulous people keen to make a quick buck. While making a decent profit is important for most landlords, especially when they have worked hard to provide a habitable property, many do have other concerns. These include the upkeep of their property, the welfare of their tenants, and concern for the environment in which they live.

Relationships between landlord and tenant tend to be more amicable and trusting when they have common interests and goals that bond them together. Concern for the environment provides such a bond, and if you, as a landlord, care about the environment and market your property to like-minded tenants, relationships will be cemented and problems reduced. Also, as environmentally friendly policy is high on the political agenda, there are a wide variety of schemes and grants available to help you to get your property habitable and save money.

This chapter offers advice on the schemes and grants available, providing information about eligibility criteria and application procedures, along with advice on sourcing green appliances, marketing your property to like-minded tenants and overcoming problems through green actions. For information about sourcing green building materials, fixtures, fittings and furnishings, consult Chapter 9.

Understanding the Green Landlords' Scheme

In 2005 the government announced its intention to encourage further investment in energy efficiency by landlords through a Green Landlords' Scheme. A scheme of this type was deemed necessary because it was acknowledged that cost savings from investing in energy efficiency are difficult for landlords to recover in increased rent.

The first part of the scheme involves additions to the landlords' energy savings allowance (LESA) which was introduced in 2004 (see below). The second part involves a review of the current wear and tear allowance which provides a deduction on taxable profits for wear and tear of furniture, fixtures and fittings. The suggestion is that this allowance should be tied in with the energy-efficiency level of the property and run alongside the new energy performance certificates (see below).

At the time of writing the government is inviting comments and discussions on the scheme to find out what improvements can be made. It is expected that further announcements will be made in the 2007 budget.

Knowing about grants and loans for landlords

There are a variety of grants and loans available for people who let property. For most grants, landlords make a direct application if they meet the eligibility criteria. However, some grants are available only for your tenants if they are in receipt of certain benefits or are classed as 'vulnerable'. If you want to take advantage of this type of grant you will need to find out whether your tenants meet the eligibility criteria and discuss whether they are happy to make an application. This type of grant is discussed in Chapter 8. Grants for which landlords can apply direct are discussed below.

The energy efficiency commitment

In the United Kingdom the government requires that energy companies fund energy improvements in domestic homes. Under the energy efficiency commitment (EEC), companies are obliged to provide grants for homeowners to install cavity wall and loft insulation.

Although it is aimed at homeowners, landlords can also take advantage of this scheme for some or all of their properties. At this present time the grant provides a £200 discount for cavity wall insulation and £150 for loft insulation. These grants are changing constantly, so for the most up-to-date information consult your local authority or your local energy efficiency advice centre (details below).

Houses in multiple occupation (HMO) grants

A house in multiple occupation (HMO) is defined as 'a house which is occupied by persons who do not form a single household'. This includes the following types of accommodation:

▊ bedsits;

▊ shared houses;

▊ hostels;

▊ lodgings;

▊ some hostels or bed and breakfast establishments;

▊ houses that have been converted into self-contained flats.

Local authorities offer discretionary grants to landlords to help them make an HMO fit for human habitation and carry out repairs or upgrade for the number of occupiers. In most areas this includes grants to improve energy efficiency, although some authorities will restrict their grants to specific improvements such as fire safety.

Some local authorities place a limit on the amount of grant available, whereas others do not have a maximum limit but the number of grants awarded is restricted by available finances. In most cases landlords have to make a means-tested contribution towards the works, based on the rent to be received from the property. Grants are not given until the required planning permissions and building regulations approval have been granted (see Chapter 10).

The property will need to continue to be let for a specified period, must be adequately insured and must be maintained in a fit condition. Some local authorities specify the rent levels that must be charged, and require the grant to be repaid in full if conditions are breached or the property is sold within a specified time. Contact your local authority for more information about this scheme.

Loan scheme for housing repairs

Some local authorities will offer loans to landlords who are wishing to repair and renovate their property. In some cases loans will be given only if the property has been deemed unfit for human habitation. The loans are interest free and repayable by landlords after a specified period, usually five years. Local authorities specify a maximum amount of loan, which could be up to £20,000, and need to approve a schedule of works before a loan will be granted. These loans are not offered in all parts of the United Kingdom. Contact your local authority for more information.

Renovation grants

Renovation grants are designed to help owner-occupiers carry out repairs or improvements to their properties. However, in some areas the grants are available for tenants, if they have a full repairing lease or a fixed-term tenancy of at least five years, and for landlords (for more information about grants for tenants, see Chapter 8). Some local authorities enable you to include energy-efficiency improvements within the works.

In most cases these grants are discretionary and will depend on the funds available. To obtain a grant you will need to hold the freehold and intend to live in or let the property for a specified number of years. Your property will need to have been classed 'unfit' for habitation or have failed the new housing health and safety rating system (HHSRS) assessment. This came into force in April 2006 in England and later in the year in Wales. It is a new risk assessment tool used to assess potential risks to the health and safety of occupants in residential properties. It replaces the housing fitness standard which was set out in the Housing Act 1985. More information about this assessment can be obtained from the DCLG (see Chapter 3).

You will not be eligible for this means-tested grant if the work can be carried out under other assistance such as an insurance or a third-party claim. Contact your local authority for more information about this grant.

Empty property grants

These grants are available to help people interested in restoring an empty property. Some local authorities will specify the amount of time that a property must have been empty before a grant will be offered, and some will offer grants only if the property is to be made available for private letting through a registered social landlord. If this is the case local authorities are very specific about the end product in terms of size of rooms, standard of accommodation, décor, fixtures and fittings, energy efficiency and heating. Once the property is renovated it must meet the criteria set out in the new HHSRS.

Local authorities will pay a percentage of the cost of works, usually in the region of 30 to 70 per cent, with most specifying an upper limit. The amount of grant you will receive depends on a number of factors including the type and size of property, its location and the intended use once the work is complete. If you sell the property or cease to let it within a specified number of years you will have to repay the grant. Contact your local authority for more information.

Knowing about tax incentives for landlords

If you are a landlord letting an individual property or a number of properties there are two schemes offering tax relief for energy-efficiency measures. These are the landlords' energy savings allowance and the enhanced capital allowance.

The landlords' energy savings allowance

The landlords' energy savings allowance (LESA) was introduced in 2004 to provide all private landlords who pay income tax with up-front tax relief on capital expenditure on energy-efficient materials. It is not available for landlords that pay corporation tax (see enhanced capital allowance below). Initially the scheme was offered for cavity wall and loft insulation, then it was extended to include solid wall insulation in rented accommodation. In April 2006 the scheme was extended further to include draught-proofing and the insulation for hot water systems.

Under this scheme you are able to deduct the cost of the new insulation when calculating your taxable profits from letting residential accommodation, up to £1,500 per property. To claim this relief you must include the expenditure as a deduction in your self-assessment tax return. This allowance is in addition to the 10 per cent deduction that HM Revenue and Customs currently allows for wear and tear of furniture, fixtures and fittings. More information about the LESA can be obtained from your local authority. The scheme is due to expire in 2009.

The enhanced capital allowance

The enhanced capital allowance (ECA) scheme was set up to encourage UK businesses to reduce carbon emissions, which contribute to climate change. This scheme provides up-front tax relief, allowing businesses to claim 100 per cent first-year capital allowances against their taxable profits. A landlord that pays corporation tax or income tax may be eligible for this scheme. This provides you with the opportunity of claiming 100 per cent of the tax back on any energy-saving technology that you buy.

ECAs are claimed in the same way as other capital allowances on the corporation tax return for companies, and the income tax return for individuals and partnerships. Only energy-saving products that meet the scheme's published energy-saving criteria can attract an ECA. For details about the current technology that meets the criteria, and for more information about the scheme, consult Chapter 9.

Producing an energy performance certificate

From June 2007 anyone wishing to sell a property must produce a home information pack which will include an energy performance certificate. Although it is intended that the certificate will be incorporated into this pack when properties are placed on the market, landlords will also need to make the certificate available to each new tenant when they let their property (see Chapter 4 for more information about home information packs).

As a landlord it is your responsibility to organize the production of a certificate, and it is estimated that the cost will be around £150. Each certificate will last for 10 years unless major renovation work is carried out. If you decide to make improvements that have an influence on the energy efficiency of your property, you can apply voluntarily for another test.

Sourcing energy-efficient white goods

The EST points out that an energy-efficient fridge freezer uses nearly a third as much energy to do the same job as a 10-year-old appliance. This means that you may be able to make a saving of £45 a year by buying an energy-efficient appliance. Through encouraging your tenants to use the washing machine on a lower temperature (30 ºC or

40 ºC) you may be able to save up to a third on electricity bills over the year. For landlords who decide to provide a dishwasher in their accommodation, a further £20 a year could be saved through buying an energy-efficient appliance, according to the EST. However, you should note that these figures are only estimates and actual savings depend on a number of related factors, such as current type and amount of usage, number of occupants, and type and condition of the existing appliance.

If the rent on the accommodation you let is inclusive of bills, buying energy-efficient white goods could help to save you up to £100 a year on electricity bills. Even if you do not include bills in the rent you intend to charge, you can advertise your property to like-minded tenants who will be impressed by the savings to be made on their utility bills over the year. It is useful to include this information in a tenants' pack that you can show to prospective tenants when they look around your property.

When you source white goods, look for the EU energy label which must, by law, be displayed clearly on all refrigeration and laundry appliances, dishwashers and electric ovens. On the top of the label the energy ratings are displayed, with 'A' the most efficient and 'G' the least efficient. Refrigeration appliances now have an 'A++' rating, which indicates exceptional energy efficiency. The label also includes information about energy consumption and running costs; washing, spinning and drying performance for laundry appliances; water consumption and capacity; and information about noise levels, although this does not have to be supplied by law.

The EST website has a database of retailers that supply kitchen appliances carrying the Energy Saving Recommended logo. This is displayed on the most efficient appliances, and means that they meet or exceed government recommendations for energy efficiency. On the website you can also find information about appliances that are specifically recommended for their energy efficiency (see Chapter 1).

Some local authorities provide grants for landlords wanting to source energy-efficient white goods. Contact your local authority or your local energy efficiency advice centre for more information about schemes in your area. You can obtain contact details of your local energy efficiency advice centre by telephoning 0800 512 012.

Marketing your environmentally friendly property

Marketing is the art of appealing to people's wants and needs in such a way that they become interested in your product or service. The green credentials of your property can give you an edge in the marketplace, helping you to charge higher rents and attract like-minded tenants who will respect and look after your property (see below). However, markets, trends and fashion change. Your marketing strategy needs to take account of this, and you need to make sure that you are able and willing to change with these fluctuations. When developing your strategy, think about the present and future conditions. Is there anything that could change your potential market in the future, and how could you respond quickly to these changes so that profits are not affected? Green issues are high on the political, public and media agenda at present, but will this be the case in the future? Will the environmental movement gain pace, and are you able and willing to update your property to keep up with these changes?

Once you have aimed your property at the green market, think about your sales strategy. Now that you know your target market, you know what will appeal – it is up to you to sell these benefits so that people are interested in your property. A competitive edge can be gained by considering the following strategies:

▌ Advertise the green credentials of your property. Choose places to advertise that are popular with environmentally aware tenants.

▌ Offer an excellent service. Follow up all enquiries efficiently, quickly and with courtesy. It is important to remain on good terms with potential tenants, especially as word of mouth is such an important free advertising tool, especially among environmentalists.

▌ Try unique packaging. When advertising your property, try something a little different. Make your property stand out to people who are interested in green issues.

▌ Emphasize the energy efficiency of your property and the savings that prospective tenants can make on their bills.

▌ Satisfy specific needs of your customers, for example by providing information about local recycling schemes, decorating with environmentally friendly materials and furnishing with natural fabrics.

■ Offer a competitive price and show your willingness to negotiate.

■ Test to modify your product. If you do not let your property quickly, invite people around for an 'open house' to find out why they are not interested. Be willing to modify your property, rent level and green strategy accordingly.

■ Develop a consistent and coherent promotion and advertising strategy. Keep records and change strategy if you are not achieving the required results.

Advertising your property can be expensive – you need to work out an effective strategy that does not cost a lot of money. Advertising on the internet can be an effective means, as can placing an advertisement in the property pages of the local newspaper or using local letting agents. Word of mouth can be one of the most effective free advertising tools. As environmental issues are high on the political and media agenda, utilize this to persuade a local journalist to write a review about your property, or write an article or advert for the local environmental group newsletter.

When potential tenants contact you, find out how they heard about your property and keep records. Over time this will show you the most cost-effective advertising strategy, and you can eliminate those that do not work so well. It is important to monitor and evaluate the effectiveness of your marketing strategy on a regular basis so that you can respond to problems and make changes as soon as they occur.

Overcoming problems through green action

Landlords face a variety of problems that arise as a result of owning property and letting to tenants. If you have bought a property and are letting it for investment purposes, it is essential that you keep it well maintained and in good condition. This will help to attract tenants, and the property will better hold or increase its value if and when you decide to sell.

As a landlord you have a legal responsibility to repair the structure and the exterior of the property. This includes maintaining and repairing drains, pipes, gutters, doors and windows. You must make sure that the installations for the supply of gas, electricity and water are maintained in a safe working order and that you have the appropriate gas and electricity test certificates. The property must be kept at a standard and fitness suitable for habitation, and meet the conditions for the new HHSRS assessment described above. For more information about your rights and responsibilities as a landlord, see *The Complete Guide to Property Development for Small Investors* (details below).

If you choose to become a green landlord and work with your tenants to make your property more environmentally friendly, you can overcome many of the problems that you already have, or may encounter, as a landlord. Some of the typical problems are listed in Table 7.1. These are followed with suggestions about the type of green action that can be taken and the benefits that can be gained by taking these steps. You may find it useful to incorporate these issues into your tenants' pack.

Summary

Environmental and ethical issues are becoming increasingly import-ant for landlords who realize that tenants with similar concerns are likely to respect and look after their property. There are a number of grants, loans and tax incentives available for landlords who wish to make energy-efficient improvements to their property, and there are schemes available to help with the purchase of energy-efficient appliances.

For landlords, an important part of developing a green property is that tenants understand the measures that have been taken, respect the landlord's environmental philosophy and look after the property in which they live. Some tenants who are in receipt of certain types of benefits are eligible to apply for grants that are not available for landlords. This type of application may be beneficial to both parties and help with the running and upkeep of the property. These issues are discussed in the following chapter.

Useful organizations

Local authorities

Your local authority is a useful source of information and advice for many aspects of residential letting and energy efficiency. Contact the housing or environmental health department for more information

Table 7.1 Overcoming typical problems

Problem	Action	Benefit
Leaking gutters and drainpipes. Damage to bricks and foundations, rotting woodwork, problems with damp.	Encourage tenants to report problems. Unblock, flush, patch, replace and/or renew gutters and drainpipes. Install water-harvesting measures (see Chapter 11).	Helps maintain structure of building by channelling water away. Saves water by harvesting. Encourages tenants to reuse water on garden. Helps foster interest in garden and helps with maintenance.
Rubbish and litter build-up. Encourages vermin, a health hazard and smelly. Causes complaints from neighbours and ill-feeling.	Provide recycling bins and compost bins with instructions. Install a covered recycling area and provide details of rubbish collection dates (see Chapters 2 and 11).	Helps environment by cutting down on waste. Stops rubbish build-up, smells, problems with vermin and complaints from neighbours. Fosters greater community spirit.
Damage to fixtures, fittings, décor and furniture through lack of respect and carelessness. At the end of the tenancy the property is left in a state of disrepair and untidiness.	Advertise for green tenants, who tend to be more responsible and careful. Encourage tenants to reuse and recycle. Provide adequate cleaning materials and tools.	Need to replace items less frequently. Saves time and money and is better for the environment. Less time, energy and money spent on cleaning and repairing. Less use of cleaning products that may be harmful to the environment.
Leaking taps and/or pipes. Water damage to property. Problems with damp and water wastage.	Encourage tenants to report problems as soon as they occur. Provide information about how to turn off the water and what tenants should do when going away. Insulate pipes and replace washers/taps where required. Check for leaks between each tenancy.	Saves water and slows limescale build-up. Prevents damage to building structure and fixtures, fittings and furniture. Saves money and time if repairs are carried out immediately.

Table 7.1 Overcoming typical problems (*continued*)

Problem	Action	Benefit
Mould and mildew growth on wood, paper, carpets and foods. Causes damage to walls, décor and soft furnishings. Looks unsightly and will put off prospective tenants. Encourages the use of strong chemicals and detergents that are harmful to the environment.	Provide information about the cause of the problem. Encourage tenants to ventilate the property and reduce indoor humidity (see Chapter 8). Repair water leaks immediately. Tackle mouldy absorbent surfaces such as ceiling tiles and carpets. Reduce condensation on cold surfaces through insulation.	Saves money through less replacement of absorbent surfaces and is kinder on the environment. Reduction means less need to use detergents and strong chemicals to tackle the problem. Tenants are less likely to experience health problems.
Complaints from neighbours about noise.	Advertise for green tenants who tend to be more responsible and respectful of others, with a greater awareness of their surrounding community. You should remain on friendly terms with neighbours and deal with problems as soon as they arise.	Creating a sense of community and developing friendships with neighbours will reduce complaints and help tenants to feel at home. It also encourages tenants and neighbours to respect and care for property in the area.
Calls from tenants 24 hours a day, often about problems they could address themselves.	Advertise for green tenants who tend to be more responsible and mature, thus dealing with problems themselves. Prepare a comprehensive tenants' pack which includes important information on which they can act without disturbing you.	Helps to maintain a good relationship with your tenants. Less time, money, fuel and energy spent on wasted journeys and telephone calls.

Table 7.1 Overcoming typical problems (*continued*)

Problem	Action	Benefit
Tenants leaving the property owing money for utility bills, council tax or telephone bills.	Advertise for green tenants who tend to be more responsible and mature. Talk to them about green tariffs and energy efficiency to reduce costs and harm to the environment (see Chapter 2). Install energy-efficient appliances to reduce costs. Encourage tenants to use energy-efficient brown goods (see Chapter 8).	Reduces problems dealing with utility companies. Reduces problems with property blacklisting and debt collectors chasing past tenants. Cuts down on letters having to be returned and stops future tenants being hassled.
Cold and draughty accommodation. Unpleasant for tenants, bad for their health and will not encourage them to respect your property.	Obtain the relevant grants to install an energy-efficient heating system and insulation before letting property. Encourage tenants to report any problems. Keep up to date with annual safety checks and supply relevant information to tenants.	Reduced energy bills, adds value to your property, encourages like-minded tenants to rent your property and helps to maintain the building. Grants help you to save money on refurbishment and renovation costs. Safety checks reduce the possibility of harm to tenants and/or contractors.

about home energy efficiency grants, renovation grants, empty property grants and the houses in multiple occupation (HMO) grant.

Many local authorities have established a landlords' forum or landlords' association. Membership is usually free and you can meet other landlords in the area to discuss energy efficiency and other relevant topics. Most produce a newsletter or other useful publications aimed at landlords.

Local energy efficiency advice centres

The EST has a network of advice centres located across England, Scotland, Wales and Northern Ireland. These centres are able to provide expert advice on energy efficiency, and information about grants and tax incentives for landlords hoping to make energy-efficient improvements to their properties. You can obtain contact details of your local centre by visiting www.est.org.uk/myhome/localadvice and entering your postcode in the box provided, or click on the relevant map location. Alternatively, you can use the form on the EST website to send an energy-related question to your local centre.

Useful websites

www.eca.gov.uk
On this website you can obtain details about the enhanced capital allowance (ECA) scheme and information about the technologies that are included within this scheme. If you prefer, you can contact the ECA Administrator (tel: 0870 190 6236, fax: 0870 190 6318, e-mail: ECAQuestions@carbontrust.co.uk).

www.hmrc.gov.uk
On this website you can obtain more information about claiming ECAs, along with information about all other tax issues.

www.livingclean.co.uk
On this website you can obtain environmentally friendly cleaning products that are based on natural products and free from harmful chemicals. The company also offers a cleaning service for landlords, using its own environmentally friendly products to clean carpets, upholstery, ovens and bathrooms.

Further reading

Dawson, C (2006) *The Complete Guide to Property Development for the Small Investor*, Kogan Page, London

Assured and Shorthold Tenancies: A guide for landlords, downloadable booklet for landlords in England and Wales, available from the DCLG website (www.communities.gov.uk)

The EST produces a number of leaflets that you may find useful. They can be ordered from the EST website (see Chapter 1) or by telephoning (0845) 120 7799:

Internal Wall Insulation in Existing Homes (CE17/GPG138)

Effective Use of Insulation in Dwellings (CE23)

Energy Efficient Refurbishment of an Existing House (CE83/ GPG155)

8 | Tenants

Some people living in rented accommodation feel that it is not possible to make many 'green' choices about where they live because these choices are constrained by the landlord and the need to find affordable, convenient accommodation. However, this is not the case. There are many small changes that tenants can make to work towards a greener way of living in rented property, and gradually more landlords are understanding the benefits that can be gained by providing more environmentally friendly accommodation.

This chapter offers advice about choosing green rental accommodation; working with your landlord to make environmentally friendly changes; understanding how to become more energy efficient in private rented accommodation; reaching consensus with other tenants; buying energy-saving brown goods; saving money through improved energy efficiency; and obtaining grants for tenants who are in receipt of benefits.

Choosing green rental accommodation

At the present time more and more landlords are realizing the benefits that can be gained from making green changes to their properties and advertising to like-minded tenants. In particular, they realize that there are financial savings to be made, that they can take advantage of a number of government grants, and that environmentally friendly tenants are more likely to respect and look after their property (see Chapter 7). This means that there are more eco-friendly rental properties on the market, and that if there are no such rental properties in your area, there may be scope to work with your landlord to improve the energy efficiency of his or her property and your home (see below).

When choosing a green property to rent, you should consider the following issues:

■ Find out about levels of rent, amount of deposit, length and type of tenancy agreement, what is included in the rent and the terms, conditions and responsibilities of you and the landlord. If you are searching for an environmentally friendly property, you might have to be prepared to pay a higher rent. However, some landlords may be willing to offer a longer contract if you can prove that you have similar green philosophies and understand the importance of looking after the property and helping the environment. This is important if you are hoping to cultivate the garden and grow your own food, as this can be a long-term project (see Chapter 11).

■ Check that the tenancy agreement meets your requirements. A tenancy agreement consists of 'express terms' that have been agreed between you and the landlord, and 'implied terms' that include the rights given by law and arrangements established by custom and practice. To avoid confusion and possible dispute your landlord should clearly state his or her responsibilities, and those expected of you, in the contract. If the landlord is interested in improving the green credentials of the property, he or she might include relevant issues within the document. You should check that you are happy with all parts of the contract before signing. The Office of Fair Trading (OFT) provides guidance on unfair contract terms in tenancy agreements, and if you believe that a contract is unfair you can report the landlord to the OFT (details below).

■ Check the inventory to make sure that it is correct and up to date. Some landlords may use an independent inventory agent who will prepare the inventory, including details of the contents, a description of their condition and information about responsibilities in terms of damage and breakages. If the landlord has sourced environmentally friendly contents, the inventory may include information about when and how these should be replaced. The inventory will need to be signed separately to the contract. More information about inventory agents can be obtained from the Association of Independent Inventory Clerks (details below).

■ Ask to see the energy performance certificate. From June 2007 all landlords must make this certificate available to each new tenant when they let their property. This will enable you and the landlord to recognize, understand and improve the energy efficiency of the property (see below).

■ Ask about the heating system that is in place. If your landlord has recently installed a new high-efficiency condensing boiler you will be able to save a significant amount of money on your gas bill each year (see below).

■ Ask to see examples of previous gas, electricity and water bills, if possible. This will help you to understand how much you have to pay each year on utilities, and it may provide an indication of where and how savings can be made. If you find that bills are high, you may be able to discuss making changes to improve energy efficiency with your landlord (see below).

■ Find out about the times and dates of local waste and recycling collection schemes, and make sure that the property has the necessary collection bins/boxes. If not, you can contact your local authority direct to obtain them. Some landlords will provide this information in a tenants' pack. This pack should also contain information on how to work the central heating, photocopies of relevant instruction manuals for washing machines, microwaves and so on, and the location of meters and stop cocks.

■ Remember that conscientious landlords are also making decisions about whether you will be a suitable tenant. Obtain references from a previous landlord if possible and take them to your viewing, although some landlords will want to follow up their own references. Think in advance about your green philosophy so that you can discuss the issues with the landlord.

Making improvements with your landlord

As a tenant you will be unable to make many improvements to the property that you rent without first seeking the permission of your landlord. If you are proposing small energy-efficient improvements such as simple draft-proofing measures, your landlord may be happy to let you go ahead on your own, but you must check that this is the case before starting any work. However, for most improvements it is sensible and preferable to work with your landlord so that both parties are happy, disagreements can be discussed and problems overcome.

It is important to establish a good rapport with your landlord. Once you have done this, and if your landlord is interested in environmental issues, it may be possible to discuss making more substantial green improvements to the property. The energy performance certificate and report will point out ways that the energy efficiency of the property can be improved, and since this must be provided by the landlord it gives you scope to discuss changes that can be made. Although financial savings tend to be made by the person living in the property, you should point out to the landlord that environmentally friendly ways of living are becoming increasingly popular, and that if he or she makes the changes, he/she should be able to let the property more quickly in future, to more responsible tenants. If your landlord pays some or all of the bills, obviously he or she will be most interested in making changes that could help him/her to save money.

Your landlord has a legal responsibility to carry out certain repairs to the structure and exterior of the property, and to make sure that gas, electricity and water supplies are in safe working order. This is a legal requirement and your landlord cannot get out of these responsibilities by adding clauses to the contract. If repairs are needed it is an ideal opportunity to suggest energy-efficient improvements, especially if a new boiler or new bathroom suite is required, for example.

You have the right to live in the property undisturbed for the period of time stated on the contract, and your landlord does not have the right to enter your home without written permission. However, you need to work with your landlord on this. All problems should be reported immediately, and it is important to allow your landlord or contractors the access required to make the repairs and improvements. When conducting repairs your landlord does not have the right to enter other parts of your home without your agreement. You will have to put up with some disruption, but if you are happy that the improvements will save you money and help the environment, the disruption should not be too much of a problem. Negotiate suitable times with your landlord for the work to take place, and you should not be disturbed more than necessary.

If your landlord agrees to have a new energy-efficient boiler installed you should discuss your needs with him or her so that the most appropriate choice can be made for you and the property. You may find it helpful to be present when the new boiler is installed. That way you can discuss operating instructions with the installer and your landlord, and make sure that you obtain a contact number in case there are any problems with the new installation. If you have built a good relationship with your landlord, he or she will be happy for you to contact the installer direct if any problems are encountered.

Although many landlords are conscientious and happy to work with their tenants to make improvements to the property, you must be aware that there are, unfortunately, some unscrupulous landlords operating. Some of these people may realize that, through making improvements to their property, they will be able to charge a higher rent. However, they cannot raise the level of rent for the duration of your tenancy agreement unless they stipulated this in the contract or they have your agreement. If they try to raise the rent without your agreement you can apply to a rent assessment committee for a decision on rent levels, especially if you believe that your landlord is trying to charge too much. This must be done before the date on which the new rent is due. More information about this procedure in England and Wales is available on the DCLG website (www.communities.gov.uk) and in Scotland from the Scottish Executive website (www.scotland.gov.uk). To find the address of your local rent assessment committee, look in the telephone book under 'rent assessment panel'.

Reaching a consensus with other tenants

For most tenants financial savings are important, and if this is the case with other people in your house you should find it fairly easy to reach a consensus about environmentally friendly changes that help you to save money (see below). However, not all environmental improvements are about saving money, and you may find it difficult to convince other people to change their habits and lifestyle if they are unable to see any personal benefits and if they don't have the same commitment as you to helping the environment.

If you are intending to rent a property with friends it should be easier for you to convince them to change their habits, as you may already have a lot in common through your existing friendship. However, if you are renting a room in a property with people you have never met before, it is much harder to discuss environmental improvements and changes. The easiest way, in these circumstances, is to choose a property in which the landlord has already tried to make green improvements. This will mean that the landlord will have screened tenants and chosen those whom he or she believes have an interest in green issues. If this is the case all tenants within the property should be able to work together to develop a household green code of action.

In some cases, however, you may rent a room in a property where the landlord and other tenants have no concern about the environment and green ways of living. If this is the case it may still be possible to convince them about the financial savings that can be made, and suggest ways that they can become more energy efficient. Most tenants will be interested in spending less money, unless they are very wealthy or careless. However, wealthy tenants tend to move on quickly and you may have better luck with the next tenant. It is possible to establish rules and routines between tenants so that any new tenant is happy to fit into these, believing them to have been long established. These could include rules about recycling, switching off lights in communal areas of the property and monitoring energy and water wastage.

If you live with other tenants who have no interest in what you are trying to do and no intention of changing their habits, it is important not to try to bully or cajole them into doing something they don't want to do. This will cause ill-feeling and lead to arguments. In these circumstances all you can do is continue with your green way of life, satisfied in the knowledge that you are doing your bit for the environment.

Becoming more energy efficient

There are many ways that you can become more energy efficient within your home, and several ways that your landlord can make your home more energy efficient. As a tenant you have responsibility for all brown goods that are not provided by the landlord, and all gas and electrical appliances that you have a right to take with you when you leave the property. You can become more energy efficient by buying energy-saving brown goods and appliances that are endorsed by the EST (see below). For a list of recommended products and suppliers, consult the EST website (see Chapter 1).

In addition to buying energy-saving goods, there is further action you can take in your home to reduce the amount of energy that you use. If you can convince other tenants to do the same, then more energy and money will be saved:

■ Take a shower instead of a bath, and persuade others to do the same. Indeed, some rental properties are now only supplied with showers.

■ Make sure all lights are switched off when not in use. Ask your landlord to fit energy-saving light bulbs, or fit them yourself. It may be possible and preferable to ask your landlord to install timed light switches in communal areas.

■ Find out whether your landlord has bought white goods that contain the energy-saving logo. If not, when goods need replacing discuss the options with your landlord and point out the benefits to be gained by buying energy-efficient white goods.

■ Make sure the insulation is adequate. The property may need cavity wall insulation, loft insulation and draught-proofing. Small jobs can be done by yourself, but you must discuss these with your landlord first. Point out that your landlord can obtain grants for wall and loft insulation (see Chapter 7). If you are on benefits you may be able to apply for certain grants for alterations to the property (see below). Again, you should discuss this with the landlord before making an application.

■ Don't leave electrical equipment on stand-by, and make sure that you have a designated responsible person who can check that all electrical equipment and heating is switched off and unplugged when tenants go away or leave the property.

■ Discuss central heating usage with other tenants. Work out the optimum time for which the heating can be programmed to come on and go off . When are people getting up in the mornings and going to bed at night? When is heat being wasted or not needed?

Buying energy-saving brown goods

'Brown goods' are items of electrical equipment that, in general, are not provided by your landlord in rented accommodation. Instead, they are items that you buy yourself and take with you when you move, such as television sets, stereos and other electrical goods.

Recently the EST included brown goods in its 'Energy Saving Recommended' scheme. At present, this includes integrated digital televisions (IDTVs) which have the capacity to receive digital television without the need for a set-top box. The switch from analogue terrestrial transmissions to digital takes place between 2008 and 2012, so the market in IDTVs is expanding rapidly. If you look for the Energy Saving Recommended logo when you make your purchase, you will be able to make small savings on the purchase price through using less electricity. More information about the switch to digital television can be found on the DTI's digital television website (www.digitaltelevision.gov.uk).

The EST also endorses energy-saving mains controllers which sense when a computer has been turned off, and automatically cut the power to any computer peripherals such as printers and speakers. The EST has found that, on average, consumers spend £700 a year on electronic products in the home, so through taking care to buy energy-efficient electronic goods, you can make savings on your electricity costs through the year. This may help you to work towards covering the costs of your electronic purchases over the long term.

To find suppliers of brown goods carrying the energy saving logo, consult the database on the EST website (see Chapter 1).

Saving money

The EST believes that a high-efficiency condensing boiler could save you in the range of £190–240 a year on your heating bills, and you could save up to £50 a year if your landlord installs floor insulation. Loft insulation, depending on the product your landlord chooses, could save you £60–70 per year on heating bills, and cavity wall insulation could save you up to £70 a year, according to the NEF. These savings, when coupled with your own energy-saving measures listed above, illustrate that you could save a considerable amount of money each year on energy bills. These savings can be used to help convince other tenants that making green changes is important. If you live with your landlord, or you rent a property inclusive of bills, these savings will appeal to your landlord and encourage him or her to continue and develop energy-saving measures.

Depending on the green changes that have been made to the property, there are other savings that can be made over the long term. For example, although a new boiler may cost your landlord £1,000–1,500 to install, you could save up to £240 a year. This means that the boiler will pay for itself after six years, and since the lifetime of a boiler could be 10–15 years, the saving over the long term is significant. Also, if your landlord decides to sell the property when your tenancy agreement has finished, more people will be willing to pay a higher price for an energy-efficient home (see Chapter 4). Again, you should note that the possible savings quoted by the EST and NEF are only estimates, and the actual savings you will make depend on a number of related factors, such as existing appliances and type of insulation, size and standard of property, number of occupants and local climatic conditions.

Obtaining grants for tenants on benefits

If you are on certain benefits and you rent your home from a private landlord there are a number of grants that may be available to you. More information about all these grants is available in the Appendix.

Home energy efficiency grants

These grants are available to help tenants and landlords to install energy-efficient heating and insulation. The grants are means-tested and available to tenants who are on means-tested benefits or low incomes. Landlords are not means-tested, but only receive a percentage of the cost of works. Schemes vary between local authorities and depend upon available funds. If funds are not available, applicants are placed on a waiting list.

Energy grants

Some local authorities offer grants to tenants who do not qualify for the type of grant mentioned above or for the Warm Front scheme mentioned below. The grants are available for various type of insulation and removal of old materials. The schemes are administered by home improvement agencies (HIA), and specific eligibility criteria apply so you should contact your local HIA for more information (see Chapter 1).

The Home Energy Efficiency Scheme (Wales)

This scheme is available for tenants who live in Wales. It is aimed primarily at households with the greatest health risks – older people, adults with children under the age of 16 and people who are disabled and chronically sick. Through this scheme a grant is provided to make homes warmer, more energy efficient and more secure.

Warm Front (England)

Through this scheme a grant is available to certain households in England. To qualify for the scheme you must rent from a private landlord, have a child under 16 or be at least 26 weeks pregnant, and be in receipt of state benefits.

Warm Deal (Scotland)

This scheme provides grants that can be put towards a number of energy-saving measures for certain households in Scotland. To be eligible for the scheme you or your spouse must rent your home, be over the age of 60 or be in receipt of state benefits. The grant will help to pay for cavity wall, loft, pipe or tank insulation, draught-proofing and energy-efficient lighting.

Central Heating Programme (Scotland)

This scheme helps certain households in Scotland to improve the heating systems in their home. To qualify for the scheme you must be resident in Scotland and rent your home, which must be your main or only residence. The property should not have a central heating system, or the present system should be broken beyond repair, and you will need to have lived in the property for at least 12 months and intend to live in the property for at least 12 months once the heating system has been installed.

Warm Homes (Northern Ireland)

Through this scheme grants are provided to improve energy efficiency for tenants who rent their homes from private landlords in Northern Ireland and are in receipt of certain benefits. Warm Homes Plus offers additional financial support for insulation measures for tenants over the age of 60 who are in receipt of certain benefits.

Summary

At the time of writing there are an increasing number of rental properties available for tenants who are interested in a greener way of life. This is because landlords and tenants are becoming more environmentally aware and realizing that there are financial savings to be made by changing habits and becoming more energy efficient. If you are able to build a rapport with your landlord and with other tenants in the property it is possible to make small and large changes that help to save money and help the environment.

Developing a more eco-friendly property is becoming increasingly important to property developers, whether or not they are also landlords, as they too can see the financial and environmental benefits to be gained. These issues are discussed in the next chapter.

Useful organizations

Association of Independent Inventory Clerks (AIIC)

AIIC was set up in 1996 to represent inventory clerks and provide information to tenants and landlords. Members must agree to abide by a code of practice. On the website you can find information about the Tenancy Deposit Scheme and details about what is meant by fair wear and tear. This is useful if you feel that your landlord is unfairly withholding your deposit.

Association of Independent Inventory Clerks
Central Office, Willow House
16 Commonfields
West End
Surrey GU24 9HZ
Tel/Fax: 01276 855388
E-mail: centraloffice@aiic.uk.com
Website: www.aiic.uk.com

Office of Fair Trading (OFT)

OFT provides useful advice for anyone who needs to draw up a contract or sign a contract drawn up by another person.

Office of Fair Trading
Fleetbank House, 2–6 Salisbury Square
London EC4Y 8JX
Tel: 08457 22 44 99
E-mail enquiries@oft.gsi.gov.uk
Website: www.oft.gov.uk

Useful websites

www.shelter.org.uk
Shelter is a housing charity that campaigns to end problems with homelessness and bad housing. Each year it helps thousands of people fight for their rights, improve their circumstances and find and keep a home. On this website you can find useful information about tenants' rights, and download leaflets and booklets about tenancy agreements, landlords' responsibility and other useful housing information.

Further reading

Callard, S and Millia, D (2001) *The Complete Book of Green Living*, Carlton Books, London
Siegle, L (2001) *Green Living in the Urban Jungle*, Green Books, Totnes
Assured and Shorthold Tenancies: A guide for tenants, downloadable booklet for tenants in England and Wales, available from the DCLG website (www.communities.gov.uk)
Private Tenancies, downloadable booklet for tenants in England from the Shelter website (details above). Information for Scottish, Welsh and Northern Irish tenants is available from the relevant national sections of the website.

9 Developers

People who are interested in property development have a great deal of scope to build, convert and/or refurbish a property in a way that matches their green philosophy. This is because environmentally friendly practices and materials can drive the development from the outset. Although undertaking a property development can be a large commitment in terms of finance, time and energy, there is the opportunity to make a good profit on a rewarding and fulfilling green project.

If you are thinking about developing a green property you need to buy appropriate land and/or buildings, assess the green potential, assess the financial potential, know what to avoid, know where and how to source green building materials and find out about grants and tax incentives for your development. These issues are discussed in this chapter.

Buying a property or land for development

As a property developer you can gain a considerable edge in the property market by buying and developing environmentally friendly commercial or residential properties. To do this successfully you need to be able to assess both the green potential and the income potential of the land and/or property.

Assessing green potential

In Chapter 3 advice is offered on recognizing the green potential of a property in which you wish to live. In addition to these points, you should ask the following questions when recognizing the green potential of property or land that you wish to develop for investment purposes, whether this is to sell or to let to tenants:

▌ What are the orientation, elevation, geography and geology of the land/property? Is there potential for harnessing wind, solar, geothermal or hydro power (see Chapter 2)? If you believe that there is potential for the installation of an alterative source of energy you will need to seek expert advice before you make your purchase, so that you can make sure there are no unforeseen problems that could arise.

▌ Is planning permission likely to be granted for the installation of renewable energy technologies? Most local authorities will look favourably on your application, but if the property is a listed building or in a conservation area, you may not be granted permission. You will also need to consider the impact on close neighbours and attempt to gauge whether they might object to your plans.

▌ What building materials have been used to construct the property? Could these be considered environmentally friendly? What materials have been used for the fixtures, fittings and décor? How time-consuming and expensive would it be to replace harmful products and materials that have been used? Would it be possible, practical and viable to replace them?

▌ What is the level and standard of existing insulation and draught-proofing? If you are new to property development, simple green improvements can be made without breaking the bank or taking a high level of risk. These simple improvements will be highlighted on the energy performance certificate that will need to be produced as part of the home information pack from June 2007 (see Chapter 4). Once you have made the improvements and your property scores a higher energy-efficiency rating, you may be able to re-market it at a higher price, although you have to be aware of movements in the local housing market to do this successfully.

Assessing income potential

To effectively assess the income potential of your green development you need to consider movement in the local market and economy in terms of present and future development, and in terms of attitudes towards environmentally friendly properties. What other development is going on the area, both by the local authority and by private developers? What are the green features of these properties and what prices are being charged? How do these differ from properties that are not considered to be environmentally friendly? How much are people willing to pay for a greener property? Consider the current market – is it buoyant? Are there plenty of estate agents in the area with strong advertising strategies? Discuss the market with estate agents to find out what is happening currently in the area, and discuss their predictions for the future, especially in terms of the local market for environmentally friendly properties. How have house prices changed over the last few years, and how do estate agents expect them to change in the future?

Speak to staff at your local planning authority and view development plans for the area in which your property is located. Find out what development is planned for the near future and how officers feel this will affect the local area. Ask about environmentally friendly policy and how this will be developed in the future, especially in terms of requirements for new property developments.

There are several ways to invest in green property. Some developers decide to utilize short-term investment opportunities, whereas others are concerned about the long-term potential. If you are interested in obtaining a buy-to-let mortgage and letting your property, you will need to think about this as a long-term investment. Although it is possible to obtain a loan for a shorter period of time, the repayments will probably exceed your rental income, and most lenders will be unwilling to lend large amounts of money in these circumstances. Refurbishing, renovating or converting a property provides the opportunity for shorter-term investment if you intend to sell the property after you have completed the work. However, if you hope to obtain a mortgage on this type of property you will have to be in a very secure financial position and be able to convince the lender that it is a viable project with profit potential. You will also have to convince the lender of your competence and reliability to carry out the required work. Green lenders will want to know that you have the knowledge and ability to make the required environmental changes.

When considering the short and/or long-term income potential on an investment, think about what is happening in the local area in terms of regeneration or degeneration. Areas that are experiencing degeneration with no sign of recovery should be avoided, whereas areas that are being regenerated, and areas adjacent to these places, may offer good investment potential. If you are intending to let your property, make sure that there are tenants available and that saturation point in the local rental market has not been reached. If you are intending to sell the property, monitor house prices and make sure that you buy in an area where the prices are rising rather than falling. Finally, you must make sure that the type of green customers to whom you are hoping to appeal are available and willing to pay the price that you ask, whether selling or letting your property.

Knowing what to avoid

There are certain properties that you should avoid if developing an eco-friendly property is important to you, especially if you are constrained financially. Although individual circumstances and properties vary considerably, in general you should think about avoiding the following types of property:

- Properties that have restrictions placed on them in terms of the development that can be undertaken. Some of these are due to the particular type of property, whereas others are to do with the area in which the property is located. The most common types of restriction are placed on listed buildings, properties in sensitive areas and through covenants in the title deeds.

- Buildings on contaminated brownfield sites. In these cases intervention may be time-consuming and costly and you would have to arrange for a commercial company to undertake the task.

- The type of ownership on a property has implications for the sort of development you are able to undertake, so you need to look into this carefully before making purchasing decisions. For example, leasehold properties may come with restrictive covenants that will influence the type of building work that you can undertake

- Land that does not have outline or full planning consent, unless you are willing to hold on to the land and take a gamble that permission will be granted at some point in the future. More information about buying land and obtaining planning permission is provided in Chapter 10.

- A property that is too expensive to convert or renovate. This may mean that you are unable to make a profit on your development or that you do not have enough finances to complete the work.

- A property that cannot be converted in an environmentally friendly way. In some circumstances it may not be possible to convert a property in the way that you want. This may be because of the existing structure and building materials, or because of difficult access, size and space in the property.

■ A green conversion that would not appeal to potential buyers. Converting some properties may have a negative visual impact which would deter the type of people who would otherwise consider making an offer.

■ Conversions that are too eco-friendly for the local market. You need to research the area and market carefully. Some people may want a more environmentally friendly home, but would be horrified at the prospect of using an outside compost toilet. People who want a very eco-friendly way of life, however, are unlikely to pay a high price for an eco-property you have developed. You need to make sure that your eco-property matches the wants and needs of your local eco-market.

■ A property with an existing boundary dispute (see below). A neighbour in dispute can make it very difficult for you to carry out your development, perhaps by opposing all planning applications or by making is difficult to access your property.

■ A property that requires more skill than your existing expertise. However, if you have the time and motivation you can consider taking part in a course or gaining experience on a different eco-build (see further reading below).

Knowing about rules and regulations

When you begin your green development you must make sure that you comply with the relevant rules and regulations. These include obtaining the necessary planning permissions, complying with building regulations, obtaining the necessary structural warranties (if new build) and arranging the right site insurance. These issues are discussed in Chapter 10.

In addition to these rules and regulations you also need to make sure that you comply with the Party Wall Act, understand boundary issues and avoid disputes with your neighbours.

The Party Wall Act

The Party Wall Act 1996 is relevant if you live in England and Wales and wish to build on an existing wall or structure shared with another property, construct a free-standing wall or the wall of a building up to or astride the boundary with a neighbouring property, or excavate within 6 metres of your neighbour's building or structure. The Act states that you must not cause unnecessary inconvenience, which includes the time when building works starts and finishes. You must provide temporary protection for any adjacent buildings and put right any damage caused by the building work.

Under the Party Wall Act you must give notice of your intentions to adjoining owners, even if the work will not extend beyond the centre line of the party wall. If you fail to provide notice, adjoining owners can stop the work by obtaining a court injunction. The best course of action is to keep on friendly terms with your neighbours and informally discuss your proposals with them. A neighbour must provide reasonable access to your workers and/or surveyor for the purpose of carrying out the work. However, you must give your neighbours at least 14 days notice if you wish to access their property. It is an offence for them to refuse access if you have followed correct procedures. Again, it is best to discuss all changes with your neighbour and point out that it is also in their interests to allow workers in, because then work can be finished properly on both sides. If the adjoining property is empty, you may gain access after following proper procedures and if accompanied by a police officer. For more information about the Party Wall Act and to find a person experienced in the workings of the Act, contact the Faculty of Party Wall Surveyors (details below).

Boundary disputes

Boundary disputes can cause problems for your development, and they are becoming more common in the United Kingdom. There are three main types of boundary dispute. The first involves high hedges, where people believe a neighbour's hedge is too high and is restricting the use or enjoyment of their property. People do not need to seek permission to grow a hedge over 2 metres in height, and the local authority will not automatically take action if the hedge is high. It will act only if it receives a complaint, and will judge each case individually. The local authority will take into account your situation, that of the hedge owner and the wider community.

The second dispute concerns locating the true position of the boundary. Boundary location disputes are incredibly hard to solve because the Land Registry is not responsible for defining boundaries and it is not possible for them to know the exact location of a boundary.

The red edging on the Land Registry title plan is not definitive and in some cases can be misleading. If a dispute should arise on a property that you wish to develop, contact the Land Registry to obtain a copy of the register entry for your neighbour's title and compare this with your own. However, if your neighbour's land is unregistered, the Land Registry will be unable to help. Even by comparing title deeds you may find that the dispute cannot be resolved. Legal definitions of boundaries are complex. If you really want to dispute the location of a boundary you will have to obtain legal advice.

The third type of dispute involves obstructed rights of way, and again you may find these disputes difficult to challenge. In some cases the right of way may have gone completely unrecorded, and although this does not mean that the right of way does not exist, it might be difficult to prove.

The best way to avoid boundary disputes is not to buy into them in the first place. When you view properties, make sure that there are no obvious boundary problems such as high hedges and blocked rights of way, and check that the boundaries you can see are the same as are registered with the Land Registry. If they don't match, think twice about buying the property. Once you have bought a property, the best way to deal with any potential boundary dispute is to remain on good terms with your neighbours and attempt to discuss and resolve any problems amicably. For more information about boundary disputes, contact your local authority or the Land Registry (details below).

Sourcing green materials

If you are intending to develop your property in an environmentally friendly way it is important to establish a list of reliable, cheap and friendly local suppliers who are able to understand and work within your green philosophy. If local suppliers are not available, you need to weigh up the environmental costs of transporting materials from a distance against the importance of sourcing green materials. This has to be an individual decision, which will be aided by an understanding of the wants and needs of your intended market. Also, if you feel that you have no choice but to transport materials over a distance, you can think about carbon offset schemes that enable you to offset your known carbon emissions by paying towards replenishing carbon stocks (see Chapter 2).

How green is your paint?

John Dison, Managing Director of earthBorn Paints, looks at the importance of paint in any green property project and unravels some of the confusion in the eco paint market.

Anyone embarking on a green property project no doubt will set out to use environmentally friendly products at every possible opportunity.

If there is one product that makes a huge difference not only to the look and feel of a property but also to the health of its occupants, the painters and the environment generally, it is paint.

The colours and finish you select superficially may be the most important factors for a completed property, but beyond that there are the hidden aspects – the health and environmental credentials – that are vital to a truly green project.

Why use eco paints?

In a nutshell, eco paints are better for your health, the environment and the building. Additionally, they represent a financial investment as properties with good eco credentials increasingly attract a premium in the property market.

Better for your health

The two main nasties in most paints are volatile organic compounds (VOCs) and acrylic softeners, both of which are given off during painting and for many years after application. It is these that produce the strong odour associated with freshly applied conventional paint, which not only is unpleasant but also causes physical reactions in some people, such as headaches and asthma attacks.

As well as being harmful to the environment, VOCs are known to cause chest complaints, aggravate allergies and cause sick building syndrome. They have also been found to be carcinogenic; painters are known to suffer a far higher than normal incidence of cancers. Acrylic softeners have been found to disrupt the body's endocrine system and impact upon fertility.

Generally, we associate high VOC levels, acrylic softeners and preservatives with oil based paints. However, they are also found in many water based paints, but not in earthBorn's wall paints or proAqua range.

Better for the environment

Let's not forget why you started your green property project!

It is widely recognised that VOCs contribute to the greenhouse effect and pollute the environment. As well as being emitted into the atmosphere during use, VOCs can find their way into the drains when washing out brushes and into groundwater from paint tins disposed of in landfill.

As part of its strategy to reduce carbon emissions, the EU has imposed maximum levels for VOCs in paint. However, these are relatively high compared to the value that environmentalists would recommend. It is far better for the environment to use paints with low, or preferably zero, VOC content.

Better for the building

The breathability of eco paint is vitally important for the fabric of a building. Contrary to the 20th century wisdom of conventional paint manufacturers who advise sealing a damp wall, eco paints work with nature, not against it.

You simply cannot seal out a damp problem for ever. Damp with nowhere to go will eventually blow the paint and plaster off the wall.

I am confident that 21st century consumers, increasingly concerned about sustainability, will find more wisdom in allowing a building to breathe. Whether it be an old wall with inherent damp problems or a newly plastered wall, letting it breathe through an eco paint will balance the humidity. In practical terms, this means less mould, better for allergy and asthma sufferers and a generally more comfortable living environment.

Traditionally, limewash was chosen if breathability was important. However, today's consumers have the choice of a more technologically advanced, highly breathable alternative – earthBorn Claypaint – which offers a wide colour choice, is more hardwearing and easier to use.

Investment

The use of environmentally friendly equipment and materials is becoming a major selling point, ask any estate agent. Investors and home buyers increasingly are interested in a property's eco credentials. Therefore, the use of eco paints can enhance the sale or rental value of your property.

What should I be looking out for?

As a relatively new phenomenon in the market place, a lot of confusion surrounds natural or eco paints. It is difficult to know what questions to ask – and how to interpret the answers you receive. So, what to look out for?

Marketing speak

First of all, a negative. Beware of woolly marketing speak such as 'traditional' and 'eco aware'; terms which are meant to give an impression of eco credentials but effectively mean nothing.

List of ingredients

Ask yourself, if a paint label does not contain a full list of ingredients, has the manufacturer got something to hide?

VOC content

Legislation requires that by the end of 2007 all paint labels carry a declaration of VOC content. The lower this value the better, but to be absolutely sure of a paint's eco credentials look out for zero VOC content.

Emissions certification
To ensure that a paint will not emit harmful chemicals once it has been applied, look out for those which are certified emission free.

Good looking
Paint is, after all, a highly visual material. It is important to find a range that offers a pleasing colour range and finish.

Practicality
While some eco paints may be good for the environment, their practicality may not compare favourably with conventional paints. However, certain modern formulations offer excellent covering power and are easy to use, long lasting, hardwearing, wipeable and anti-static.

The definitive symbol
The most reliable method of ensuring you buy a truly eco friendly paint is to look for the EU Ecolabel or a paint manufactured by a member of ENAP (the European Association of Natural Paint Producers).

Europe's definitive environmental standard, Ecolabel certifies that products make minimal impact on the environment throughout their life cycle – during manufacture, use and disposal – and do not harm the health of people using or living with them.

For further information visit
www.defra.gov.uk/environment/consumerprod/ecolabel

On our website you'll find tables that offer a useful comparison of products from the earthBorn range and other paints on the market.

For further information, please visit our website **www.earthbornpaints.co.uk**

Green building materials

The tips below will help you to think more about sourcing green building materials:

▌ Plan your refurbishment or new build carefully. Think about the environmental impact of your project and the materials that you intend to use. Plan ahead, seeking appropriate advice from professionals if you feel that you lack the appropriate knowledge and/or experience. Contact details for a variety of professionals who are interested in green building issues can be obtained from the Green Register (details below).

▌ Use recycled timber where possible. If this is not possible or practical, check that timber is locally grown or FSC accredited (see below).

▌ Try to use durable timber species for external work as this will reduce the need to use so much wood preserver. English oak, sweet chestnut and European larch are good examples of the type of durable timber that can be used for external construction.

▌ Choose formaldehyde-free chipboard and MDF. If this is not possible choose birch plywood, high-density fibreboard or Sterling board, which have much lower formaldehyde content.

▌ If you are unable to source locally grown timber or other building materials, because of cost or availability, think about carbon offset schemes to cover emissions from transit (see Chapter 2).

▌ Choose materials that are natural and from a renewable source.

▌ Don't immediately be put off by higher prices for natural materials – sometimes initial higher capital expenditure can be offset against lower operating costs. You will also cut down on transport and delivery charges if you can source locally grown/produced materials.

▌ Use natural insulation materials as these don't contain harmful chemicals. Natural products may be made from fire-retarded, recycled newspapers or from British sheep's wool.

For information about a wide range of products that promote energy efficient, sustainable and healthy buildings, consult the Green Building Store website (details below).

Established in 1995, Tŷ-Mawr is a successful family business run from an old stone farmhouse on the shore of Llangorse Lake in the Brecon Beacons National Park.

Tŷ-Mawr specialises in environmentally friendly building products, particularly lime-based mortars and plasters. These require less energy to manufacture than their cement based equivalents and, just as importantly, are fully recyclable.Tŷ-Mawr is particularly popular with buildings conservation specialists, their products are used on restoration projects throughout the country. Their insulated "limecrete" flooring system has been used to replace the floor of the Chapter House at Worcester Cathedral, and for the rebuilding of a 13th century church at the National Museum of Wales in Cardiff. It is an ideal alternative to concrete in older buildings and is becoming popular in ecological new builds.

Though enthusiasts of traditional building techniques the Gervis's are not by any means Luddites. They do innovation to. Alarmed by the environmental effects of large scale sand extraction Joyce and Nigel decided to find an alternative aggregate for their product range. The result is "Glaster™", a range of products in which crushed recycled glass is used instead of sand.

The different grades and colours of glass used produce a unique and beautiful aesthetic for internal and external walls. Architects Adams and Collingwoood chose "Glaster™" to render the exterior of their new premises West London.

Tŷ-Mawr Lime has taken the best of traditional materials and given them a contemporary 'twist'; not for the sake of it, but because they are concerned about the impact buildings have on the environment. As a nation Britain consumes 6 tonnes of building materials per person per annum but Joyce and Nigel Gervis believe that by choosing our building materials carefully, we can all greatly improve our environmental footprint.

www.printsofwales.biz

Text and photos by Jim Saunders

Green fixtures, fittings, furnishings and décor

The tips below will help you to think more about sourcing green fixtures, fittings, furnishings and décor:

■ Buy environmentally friendly paints that are derived from plant and mineral ingredients. Most manufacturers will be happy to supply you with samples and a comprehensive list of ingredients for their paints. If you want to use a painter or decorator who uses this type of product, search the Association for Environment Conscious Building (AECB) database for contact information (details below).

■ Think about using lime washes instead of paints containing harmful chemicals or that have been produced in a way that harms the environment.

■ Where possible, avoid or limit the use of products that contain volatile organic compounds (VOCs). These are emitted as gases from certain solids and liquids and can pollute the indoor and outdoor atmosphere, contribute towards global warming and lead to health problems, especially for people who suffer with breathing difficulties. Products that contain VOCs include certain paints, wood preservers, cleaning products, cosmetics, furnishings, office equipment such as printers and copiers and injected damp-proof courses. More information about these issues can be obtained from the Environment Agency website (www.environment-agency.gov.uk).

■ Reduce synthetic chemical usage and use natural fabrics and furnishings. It is generally believed that the increasing number of allergies and cases of hypersensitivity are caused by an overload of synthetic chemicals. However, some products that are marketed as 'hypoallergenic' may not be the most environmentally sensitive on the market. You will have to use your judgement when sourcing this type of product. An online catalogue of products that help to relieve allergies is available at www.healthy-house.co.uk.

■ Use wood finishes that are based on natural oils and waxes. These will penetrate the wood and keep it elastic and healthy. They will also repel water and are highly durable. A full range of internal and external wood finishing products is available from the Green Building Store (details below).

▌ Choose water-efficient WCs, flow regulators for taps on baths and showers, or water-saving cartridges for taps that save water and energy.

Knowing about grants and tax incentives

There are a number of grants and tax incentives that you can take advantage of for your property development, as listed below. More information about all these grants and schemes can be found in the Appendix.

The enhanced capital allowance

The enhanced capital allowance (ECA) scheme was set up to encourage UK businesses to reduce carbon emissions which contribute to climate change. This scheme provides up-front tax relief, allowing businesses to claim 100 per cent first-year capital allowances against their taxable profits. If you are a property developer who pays corporation tax or income tax, you may be eligible for this scheme. Only energy-saving products that meets the scheme's published energy-saving criteria can attract an ECA. The technologies that currently appear on the Energy Technology List and are therefore eligible for the ECA are listed in Appendix 1. HM Revenue and Customs (HMRC) administers claims and will check for negligent or fraudulent claims. More information about making a claim can be obtained from the HMRC website (details below).

Local authority schemes

Local authorities throughout the United Kingdom offer some grants and loans for developers hoping to improve their property. However, most will specify that you must live in or let the property for a specified number of years after the development has taken place, so these grants may not be suitable if you intend to sell the property once developed. Eligibility criteria vary between local authorities and will depend on the grant or loan for which you are applying. Local authority schemes vary from year to year, depending on the funds available, so contact the housing section of your local authority to find out what is available. Many now publish details of their grants on their website or publish an information leaflet on 'housing grants' or 'energy-efficiency grants'.

Home energy efficiency grants

These grants are available to help owner-occupiers, landlords and tenants to install energy-efficient heating and insulation. The grants are means-tested and available to homeowners and tenants who are on means-tested benefits or low incomes. It may be possible for a developer to obtain these grants if you intend to let your property to vulnerable tenants. Landlords are not means-tested, but only receive a percentage of the cost of works. Schemes vary between local authorities and depend upon available funds. If funds are not available applicants are placed on a waiting list.

Renovation grants

Renovation grants are designed to help owner-occupiers carry out repairs or improvements to their properties. However, in some areas the grants are available for tenants, if they have a full repairing lease or a fixed-term tenancy of at least five years, and for landlords and developers if they intend to let their property to vulnerable tenants. Some local authorities enable you to include energy efficiency improvements in the works. To obtain a grant you will need to hold the freehold and intend to live in or let the property for a specified number of years. Your property will need to have been classed 'unfit' for habitation or failed the new Housing Health and Safety Rating System (HHSRS) assessment which came into force in April 2006 in England.

Empty property grants

These grants are available to help people interested in restoring an empty property. Local authorities will pay a percentage of the cost of works, usually in the region of 30–70 per cent, with most specifying an price upper limit, usually around £10,000. The amount of grant you will receive depends on a number of factors, including the type and size of property, its location and the intended use once the work is complete. If you sell the property or cease to let it within a specified number of years, you will have to repay the grant. Some local authorities will specify the amount of time that a property must have been empty before a grant will be offered, and some will only offer grants if the property is to be made available for private letting through a registered social landlord. If this is the case, local authorities are very specific about the end product, in terms of size of rooms, standard of accommodation, décor, fixtures and fittings, energy efficiency and heating. Once the property is renovated it must meet the criteria set out in the new HHSRS.

Loan scheme for housing repairs

Some local authorities will offer loans to homeowners, landlords and developers who are wishing to repair and renovate their property. In some cases loans will only be given if the property has been deemed unfit for human habitation. The loans are interest free and repayable by homeowners either when the property is sold or bequeathed, or in the case of landlords, after five years. Local authorities specify a maximum amount of loan, which could be up to £20,000, and need to approve a schedule of works before a loan will be granted. Homeowners should check whether this is the most suitable method of raising finances, as, in the event of their death, relatives will need to pay back the loan, whether or not they sell the property.

Houses in multiple occupation (HMO) grants

An HMO is defined as 'a house which is occupied by persons who do not form a single household'. Local authorities offer discretionary grants to landlords to help them make an HMO fit for human habitation, or carry out repairs or upgrade for the number of occupiers. This includes grants to improve energy efficiency. In most cases landlords/developers have to make a means-tested contribution towards the works, based on the rent to be received from the property. Grants are not given until the required planning permissions and building regulations approval have been granted. The property will need to continue to be let for a specified period of time, must be adequately insured and must be maintained in a fit condition. Some local authorities specify the rent levels that must be charged, and require the grant to be repaid in full if conditions are breached or the property is sold within a specified period.

Low Carbon Buildings Programme

Through the Low Carbon Buildings Programme individual house-holders can apply for grants to help with the installation of renewable sources of energy for their homes. Larger grants are available for communities that decide to install renewable energy technology for community use. For property developers there may be conditions attached to these grants, so you should check eligibility criteria before making your application.

Scottish Community and Householder Renewables Initiative

The Scottish Community and Householder Renewables Initiative offers grants and advice to people in Scotland who wish to develop renewable sources of energy. It is possible for builders, developers and architects to apply for grants on behalf of future owners of houses they are building. To qualify for a grant you must own the property where the renewable energy system is to be installed, you must obtain a quotation from an accredited installer and you must use an approved installer using an approved system.

Summary

If you are hoping to develop a property to let to tenants or to sell on for a profit, you have considerable scope for making green improvements and working within your green philosophy. With careful research and planning you can make sure that you choose the right plot of land and/or property and that you source environmentally friendly materials that meet the expectations of your intended market.

As with all property development you need to make sure that you comply with the relevant laws and legislation. This is of particular importance if your development involves large extensions or new build. Issues that are of concern to people who are thinking about building their own house are discussed in the next chapter.

Useful organizations

Faculty of Party Wall Surveyors

Members of the Faculty of Party Wall Surveyors are experienced in the proper workings of the Act. They can be employed to serve the appropriate notices for you and see that the Act is properly implemented.

Faculty of Party Wall Surveyors
19 Church Street
Godalming
Surrey GU7 1EL
Tel: 01424 883300
Fax: 01424 883300
E-mail: enq@fpws.org.uk
Website: www.fpws.org.uk

Association for Environment Conscious Building (AECB)

AECB is a network of individuals and companies with a common aim of promoting sustainable building. On the website you can find information about improving the environmental performance of your property, choosing eco-friendly products and avoiding damaging chemicals, using timber, and planning and developing eco-friendly properties.

Association for Environment Conscious Building
PO Box 32
Llandysull SA44 5ZA
Tel: 0845 456 9773
E-mail: graigoffice@aecb.net
Website: www.aecb.net

Useful websites

www.landregisteronline.gov.uk
Land Register Online provides easy access to details of more than 20 million registered properties in England and Wales. You can

download copies of title plans and registers in PDF format for £3 each, payable online by credit card.

www.eca.gov.uk

On this website you can obtain details about the enhanced capital allowance (ECA) scheme, and information about the technologies that are included within this scheme. If you prefer, you can contact the ECA Administrator (tel: 0870 190 6236, fax: 0870 190 6318, e-mail: ECAQuestions@carbontrust.co.uk).

www.hmrc.gov.uk

On this website you can obtain more information about claiming ECAs, along with information about all other tax issues.

www.fsc.org

The Forest Stewardship Council (FSC) is an international network that promotes the responsible management of the world's forests. It has an accreditation and labelling scheme through which purchasers can ensure that their timber comes from forests that meet FSC standards.

www.greenbuildingstore.co.uk

This is the website of the Green Building Store, which is owned and run by Environmental Construction Products Ltd. This company has specialized in environmentally sensitive building products since 1995, and is committed to energy-efficient, sustainable and healthy buildings. On the website you can search the full product range for glazing, guttering, insulation, paints and wood finishes, sanitary ware, taps and water-saving products, timber preservation, water-efficient WCs, and windows and doors.

www.greenregister.org

The Green Register is a training and networking organization for professionals who are interested in sustainable building issues, including architects, builders, surveyors, engineers and tradespeople. You can access the Green Register by geographical location, and full contact details of members are provided.

www.salvoweb.com

Salvo is a partnership that aims to support dealers who hold stocks of architectural salvage, reclaimed building materials, demolition salvage and recycled materials. Where possible it encourages fair trade and eco-friendly activities. Contact details for dealers, suppliers and craftspeople can be obtained from the website.

Further reading

Dawson, C (2006) *The Complete Guide to Property Development for the Small Investor*, Kogan Page, London

Harland, E (1999) *Eco-Renovation: Ecological home improvement guide*, Resurgence Books, London

Plowright, T (2007) *Eco-centres and Courses*, Green Books, Totnes

10 Self-builders

Self-build is becoming more popular, and one of the reasons for this popularity is more demand for eco-friendly ways of living. New houses provide this opportunity as they can be built with energy efficiency in mind, with good insulation, energy-saving devices and lower running costs. It is now possible to obtain a new-build mortgage which provides some of the finance up front so that you don't have to sell your existing home or move into rented accommodation while you are building your property. Also, there are some good government incentives and tax savings available for new-build projects.

This chapter provides information on buying land for a new house, obtaining planning permission, working within building regulations, planning and designing your house, purchasing environmentally friendly materials, using sustainable energy sources and obtaining grants and tax incentives.

Buying land

There are four main ways to buy land, and the method that you choose will have an influence on the price and the likelihood of your obtaining planning permission for your green project.

Buying land with full planning permission

The easiest way to buy land on which you know that you will be able to build is to buy a plot that already has planning permission, as in most cases planning permission runs with the land and not with the applicant (you should check that this is the case before purchasing). However, the drawback is that this type of plot will be much more expensive than other land, and the plans for the building will already have been drawn up, so you will have little input into the structure and design of the property. While it may be possible to make minor changes without permission, or receive approval for some alterations, you will generally have to follow the original plans and these may not match your wants, needs and green philosophy. If you decide to make any changes to original plans, you must seek advice first.

However, this type of land purchase is the easiest option as you know that plans have already been approved, so you save yourself considerable time and worry over submitting plans yourself. Also, as eco-friendly new-build is high on the political and public agenda, if you conduct careful research and take your time, you may be able to find a plot with plans that meet your green requirements.

Buying land with outline consent

Another way that building plots are sold is with outline consent. This means that, in principle, a development will be acceptable on the plot. However, you will need to submit a full planning application and it if differs greatly from the scheme put forward for outline consent, success is not guaranteed. Land with outline consent is cheaper than land with full planning permission, but more expensive than land without any type of permission.

Buying land without planning permission or consent

By far the cheapest way to buy land is without planning permission or consent. However, buying land for building in this way is a big gamble because you do not know whether permission will ever be granted to build your house. You must conduct careful research before choosing this option. In particular, you will need to make sure that there are no strings attached to the purchase of the land, as some will stipulate no development or that the land must remain for agricultural use.

It is important to have an informal chat with your local planning authority, as its staff will be able to give you a general idea whether permission would ever be granted on the plot. You can also view the development plans for your local area, which will give you a better idea of whether there is a possibility that planning permission may be granted. Information about local development plans can be obtained from the planning portal (details below). If an area is already being developed, you may stand a better chance of receiving planning approval, whereas it is much harder to receive approval in areas such as conservation areas or those with a vocal, active community against development. However, the green credentials of your proposed building may help to convince people that your project will not harm the environment or be an eyesore.

Buying land with an existing building

It is possible to buy land with an existing building that could be demolished, or altered considerably, to produce your own eco-friendly building. If you choose this option you will need to conduct careful research to find out whether you are able to demolish the existing building. If the building is listed, located in a conservation area or has been issued with a building preservation notice, you will need listed building and/or conservation area consent before you undertake any work, and it is not guaranteed that consent will be given. It is an offence to demolish, alter or extend a listed building without listed building consent, and the penalty can be a fine of unlimited amount, imprisonment or both. You will also need to make sure that the local authority has not made an Article 4 directive restricting the demolition or alterations that you could normally make under permitted development rules. More information about listed buildings and conservation areas can be obtained from the English Heritage website (www.english-heritage.co.uk).

For all demolition of residential property you must seek advice from your local planning authority before work starts. You will need to agree details of how you intend to carry out the demolition or alterations and how you propose to restore the site afterwards. You will need to apply for a formal decision about whether your plans are approved – this is called a 'prior approval application'. More information about making this application can be obtained from your local planning authority.

You will have to apply for planning permission on all new buildings or alterations that you are proposing, and you will need to find out whether you have to use the same footprint of the building you intend to demolish. All permission should be sought before any work begins as, even if the building is fire or storm damaged, or dilapidated, planning permission approval is not guaranteed.

Finding land for sale

Finding the right plot can take a long time. You will need to be patient and conduct careful, detailed research. Use the websites listed below to start your search, and build up a list of useful estate or land agents who can help you to find a plot. Alternatively, you can use a land agent to do the work for you. He or she will take a cut of the price you pay for the land, so you will need to agree terms and make sure that the price and service are acceptable. If you use an experienced and knowledgeable land agent he or she will be able to find the right type of plot and offer advice about the likelihood of planning permission being granted. Building plots and land agents can be found from the Building Plot website (www.building-plot.org.uk), but care must be taken when choosing land or an agent and it is advisable to seek legal advice from a well-qualified professional.

Obtaining permission

If you have chosen to purchase land without planning permission, or you already own land on which you would like to self-build, you will need to obtain planning permission.

Obtaining outline consent

One way to find out whether you have a chance of your plans being approved without spending a great deal of money drawing up intricate plans is to put in an application for outline consent. This is a form of planning consent designed to test the principle of whether or not a new development is acceptable. When you submit an application for outline consent, the planning authority can request as much information as it requires in order to make an informed decision. However, decisions about materials, style, design and landscaping will not have to be made at this point.

Obtaining full planning permission

If you decide to make a full application you will need to draw up detailed plans of your proposed building. This will need to include the size, layout, position and external appearance of the building.

You will also need to consider issues of access, landscaping and the impact on the local neighbourhood. The planning authorities will want to know about existing infrastructure, including roads and water supplies, and how your proposed building will fit into this. You must also include information about the proposed use of the building. If eco-design is important to you, the application should include comprehensive details of your plans, especially if you intend to generate your own energy and/or limit carbon emissions, as this may help your application.

Making a planning application

Before you make an application, get in touch with your local planning authority – contact details can be obtained from the planning portal (see below). Speak to staff about what you intend to do and seek their advice. You can also find out whether there are any anticipated problems and discuss possible ways to overcome them.

Application forms can be obtained from your local planning authority, or you can make your planning application online through the planning portal (details below). If your plans are refused it is possible to revise them and submit a new application, or you could make an appeal (see below). If your plans have been approved, generally you can start work straight away, but you should check that you don't need other approvals such as conservation area consent before you begin work. All work must start within three years or you will be required to apply again for permission.

Making an appeal

You have the right to appeal against all planning refusals. To do this you need to put together all the facts into a written statement, which is then sent to the Planning Inspectorate in Bristol. An inspector is appointed to read through all submissions, visit the site and decide whether the council should have approved the application. The process may take up to four months. Appeals in England must be submitted within six months of the refusal. For more information about making an appeal, contact the Planning Inspectorate (details below).

Using chartered building surveyors

If this is the first property you have built and the first time you have prepared a planning application, you may find it useful to enlist the help of an experienced chartered building surveyor. He or she will work with you to find out exactly what you want and discuss whether it will be both possible and permissible, helping you to maximize the potential of your site and work within your green requirements. Chartered building surveyors can also help with the preparation of plans suitable for Building Regulations purposes (see below). To find a chartered building surveyor in your area, contact the Royal Institute of Chartered Surveyors (RICS) (details below).

Understanding rules, regulations and procedures

There are a variety of rules, regulations and procedures that you will need to understand and follow when you build your own house. These include Building Regulations approval, structural warranties, appropriate insurance, and health and safety legislation.

Building Regulations approval

Before you begin any work on a new building you must obtain Building Regulations approval. If you carry out work without the required approval you could face prosecution. Building Regulations can be complex, and if you are in doubt you should make sure that you receive the appropriate advice specific to your project before you begin work. This could be from an architect, building surveyor or structural engineer.

During construction the building work is checked at various stages to make sure that it complies with Building Regulations and is in accordance with the approved plans. From April 2006 new rules state that part of this assessment must include air pressure leakage testing, and new dwellings must meet a minimum overall energy performance standard in terms of a target carbon dioxide emission rate. Written records are made during each inspection, and if there are any problems they are raised with the builder and/or the applicant. Follow-up inspections are made if any remedial work is needed. If the work is completed satisfactorily a completion certificate is issued at the end of the job. This certificate will be required when you decide to sell or remortgage your property, and should be included in your home information pack (see Chapter 4).

To apply for Building Regulations approval on a new property you will need to make a full plans application. All application forms can be obtained from your local planning authority or downloaded from its website. Alternatively, you can use the government public services website to enter your postcode and be directed to the relevant authority website (www.direct.gov.uk). A full plans application needs to contain detailed drawings of the proposed building work; site or location plans, detailing site boundaries and the position of public sewers; fire safety drawings, where required; copies of the structural design and calculations; an application form and appropriate fee. The application form should be completed fully and accurately, with all the necessary paperwork attached, as this will help your application to run smoothly and avoid delays. A decision is usually issued within five weeks, although it may take up to eight weeks in some circumstances.

Structural warranties

Every new home needs a structural warranty to protect its owner against the risk of latent defects. Although it is not a mandatory requirement, you should take out a warranty as you will find it very difficult to sell your home within the first 10 years of construction without one. This is because mortgage companies will not offer a mortgage to potential buyers on a property under 10 years old without a warranty, whatever its green credentials.

In the UK the largest warranty provider is the National House-Building Council (NHBC), and two of its schemes are suitable for self-builders – Buildmark and Solo. More information about these schemes can be obtained from the NHBC website (www.nhbc.co.uk). Other warranties that are suitable for self-build include Zurich's 'Newbuild' and 'Custombuild' warranties (www.zurich.co.uk) and the Self-Builder Structural Guarantee (www.self-builder.com).

Site insurance

When you decide to self-build you must protect yourself, your employees and your investment by arranging suitable site insurance. Your site insurance should cover the following:

- the existing structure, if there is one, and new work against such losses as fire, theft, flood, storm damage, vandalism and accidental damage;

- building works, temporary works and materials;

- your own and hired plant, tools and equipment;

- residential caravans, site huts, containers and contents;

- employees' tools and personal effects;

- employer's liability, which will cover you if anything happens to anyone working on your site;

- public liability, which will cover you if anything happens to anyone visiting your site;

- legal expenses cover , which will help you if a dispute arises with professionals, local authorities, suppliers or contractors;

- personal accident insurance;

- optional building insurance.

If you place a single contract with a builder, architect or eco-specialist, he or she should arrange appropriate insurance, but you must check that this is the case before work starts.

Health and safety legislation

Minimum standards are laid down by law in the interests of health and public safety. They are there to protect you and your family from unsound work that could place you in danger. Contravention of these laws can lead to prosecution and the possible imposition of substantial fines. Before you begin any of the work yourself, you must find out about these minimum standards. Some work on your property can only be carried out by an installer or tradesperson who is registered with the appropriate government-approved body.

Always be aware of the health hazards attached to any work you intend to carry out yourself. Conduct a risk assessment before you begin the work. This involves making judgements about the level of risk involved and deciding what you can do to reduce the risk to an acceptable level. If this is your first project you may find it useful to seek the advice and guidance of a fully qualified professional. More information about health and safety can be obtained from the Health

Timeless Style
Sophisticated Elegance

HUF HAUS post and beam architecture, using only the highest quality materials, is pure fascination. Exclusive high ceiling rooms, roof glazing, bright unique living combined with a first class finish and individual planning down to the smallest detail – and all from a one-stop shop. Experience our contemporary wood and glass design concept at first hand by contacting us on
Tel: 0870 2000 035,
Fax: 0870 2000 036.
Alternatively visit our website at www.huf-haus.com or email us at london@huf-haus.com

 **HUF HAUS**

homes by design

Prices starting from £300,000

Homes by Design

Have you ever dreamed of a home with space, a modern and opulent design, that also offers spectacular views of beautiful and natural landscapes? Then maybe your dream home could just be a HUF house.

The defining hallmark of a HUF home is its post and beam design, which offers architecture that creates an open flowing living space. Floor to ceiling glazing and glass gables reveal the surrounding natural environment, drawing it into the living experience.

The History

The HUF HAUS company, based in the Westerwald, Germany, is a recognised leader throughout Europe for the design and the construction of timber and glass buildings. Due to the ever evolving product range and its bespoke and client orientated concept, the company has enjoyed continuous growth for over ninety years. The course was set for success during the late 1960s in Hartenfels, Germany, when the decision was made to market pre-fabricated detached houses. Less than ten years later the company developed the POST & BEAM HOUSE 2000 and the basic principles are still adhered to in all HUF houses today. As a result, the combination of timber and glass gives HUF houses their distinctive look.

The Concept

A HUF home evolves from its early design stage, which is kick started with an initial site visit, then moves into its design and planning stages, followed by a Fit-out meeting in Germany, where all clients can choose from a vast range of fixtures, fittings, flooring, lighting, built-in furniture, bathrooms and kitchens. Once the interior has been agreed, the production of the individually tailored HUF house can begin.

The site is prepared and awaits the arrival of the new building, which is transported from Germany and is assembled on site in just one week. The interior is then fitted and completed by the HUF team within 12 weeks, depending on the size of the project.

The option of a basement has proven very popular and cost effective, especially with clients who require additional living rooms, storage space, utility rooms, or even media rooms and guest accommodation.

Fact File

HUF HAUS offers many benefits to the homebuyer, from individual design to the efficiency of its building process.

- The Structural system used is centuries old and is tried and tested, based on the post and beam method. This type of construction eradicates the need for load bearing walls, allowing large, open spaces to be created internally. All walls and glazed areas are infills and can be altered easily to suit your needs.

- HUF HAUS provides a complete house which includes the heating, wiring, and concrete screed to all floors, carpet, tiles, sanitary ware, blinds and decorating. The package includes the professional advice of an architect, who will visit your site and discuss the design of your home, and an in-house planning consultant managing the required planning applications.

- The building process is kept to a minimum. Landscaping the site can start after the first week, reducing the time the site is an eye sore.

- Heat efficiency in a HUF house is a very high priority. HUF HAUS achieves a SAP (Standard Assessment Procedure) rating of between 95 and 117, which is the highest achievable rate in the UK.

- Recently studies have shown that the air tightness of a HUF house is one of the highest achievable in this country.

Costs

As each house is tailor made, prices will vary. Prices start from £130 per square foot, excluding groundworks, kitchen and light fittings, and for the basement you should allow a starting price of £75 per square foot. The whole process from start to finish takes 14 months subject to planning.

and Safety Executive Information Line: (0845) 345 0055 or from its website (www.hse.gov.uk).

Planning and designing

Unless you are an experienced planner or designer it is advisable to work with a professional when you begin to develop and design your new home. There are three main ways that you can do this. The first is to work with an architect who can help to put your ideas on paper, advising whether they are feasible, practical and possible within your budget. The second is to work with an eco-design specialist, such as a building company, a manufacturer or an experienced individual. The third method is to construct your own eco-house using one of the kits available on the market.

Working with an architect

An architect can advise you on planning permission, Building Regulations, health and safety, eco-design, and deal with the authorities on your behalf. If you decide to employ an architect you will need to agree on the scope and cost of architectural services before the project is started. Think about how much of an architect's services you wish to use, from an initial design discussion through to full completion of the project. All negotiations should be agreed in writing, and you should develop a good working relationship with your architect.

Architect's fees can be based on a percentage of the total construction cost, on the amount of time taken for the project or on an agreed lump sum. When choosing an architect ask for a breakdown of the fees involved. You should speak to several architects to find out what services they can offer and the prices they charge. For more information about choosing and working with an architect, contact the Royal Institute of British Architects (details below).

Working with an eco-design specialist

Companies, manufacturers or individual professionals that specialize in eco-design often offer a complete plan, design and supply service, which means that you do not have to employ a separate architect, designer or builder. If you choose a reliable and competent company or individual you can save yourself considerable time and effort, as they will also be able to offer advice about planning permission and building regulations. You can work with the specialist to make sure that the design of the property meets your wants, needs and green requirements.

When choosing an eco-design specialist, use the relevant trade or membership association to find a fully qualified and legitimate individual or company, such as the UK Timber Frame Association or Straw Bale Building Association (see below). You can also use the Self Build Package Company Directory on the Build Store website to obtain contact details of organizations in your area (details below). Try to make choices based on personal recommendations, references and evidence of previous work. Ask about qualifications, experience, warranties and insurance. Get to know the specialist and make sure that you can work happily with him or her. In particular, make sure that he or she understands, and can work within, your green philosophy.

Working with an eco-kit

If you are an experienced builder, or very competent in DIY, it is possible to purchase a house in kit form and construct the property yourself. If you choose this option you must have the required level of skill and conduct thorough research into the type of kits available. Kits come with drawings specific to each kit and a builder detail book that shows how it all fits together and what else you will need to purchase to complete your building.

In general, kits are loaded by forklift truck onto an articulated lorry, so you will need to make sure that the vehicle can access your site and that you hire a forklift truck to unload the kit. The Timber Frame Association provides a useful starting place for your research (details below). If you want to improve your skills and learn more about building your home, details of courses can be obtained from the Walter Segal Self Build Trust website (www.segalselfbuild.co.uk). More information about all aspects of self-build can be obtained from the self-build website (details below).

IF ONE SINGLE TREE CAN ABSORB FIVE TONS OF CO_2, THEN JUST THINK WHAT A WHOLE TIMBER HOUSE CAN DO.

At least fifty tons of carbon dioxide are stored in every Baufritz home, rather than being released into the atmosphere where they would add to the damaging greenhouse effect. That's more CO_2 than a modern family car produces, driving an average of 6,000 miles a year for twenty years. We call this CO_2 positive. It is only one of the ways that we are working to reduce the long-term carbon footprint of every new Baufritz home. Energy efficient heating systems, solar panels, and state-of-the-art insulation, all help to ensure that the homes we build not only benefit the environment now, but also bring benefits to you for years to come.

Baufritz (UK) Ltd, The Workplace, Oakington Road, Girton, Cambridge CB3 OQH, www.baufritz-gg.com, Phone: 01223 235632

CO_2 POSITIVE

BAUFRITZ
SEIT 1896

Natural building innovation

Established in 1896, Baufritz is a multi award winning pioneer in ecological timber house construction. With its headquarters in Germany, and a UK office in Cambridge, Baufritz offers stunning, high quality, tailor-made homes which provide a healthier way of living and an eco friendly building approach. As Baufritz uses highly efficient modern methods of construction, the initial structure of a Baufritz home (a water tight shell incorporating walls, doors, windows and the roof) can be constructed in as little as one to two days. The average Baufritz home is usually completed in around 9 months from planning and design right through to completion, which is around a third of the time it takes to build an ordinary brick and mortar house.

As timber is the only renewable building material, it means that owners of a Baufritz house will be helping to preserve nature's cycle. Baufritz has gone beyond being 'Carbon Neutral' and is one of the few firms that started building 'Carbon Positive' homes some 15 years ago. Baufritz combines sustainable ecology and the highest energy efficiency in all its buildings.

Fossil fuels and their application are becoming increasingly important with regards to climate protection. Timber for example, is able to store vast amounts of carbon dioxide which is absorbed from the atmosphere during photosyntheis while the tree is still alive. Every Baufritz house is carbon positive to the extent that each house stores at least 50 tonnes of carbon dioxide; the equivalent of a family saloon car doing 6,200 miles per year, every year for 20 years. Baufritz was the first German construction company to take the independent 'EU Eco Audit' in 1996, which it has passed four times to date.

Only the best quality organically grown Larch and Spruce wood go into making a Baufritz home, logged from sustainable forests to provide resource for future generations. Baufritz undertakes extensive tree planting schemes to mark its active approach to environmental protection. Each home built by Baufritz comes with a unique promise; because the materials used to build it are 100% biodegradable, the home can be completely returned to nature in several generations if required. Baufritz also implements an environmentally friendly approach to powering its homes by advocating renewable energy sources such as geothermal energy and solar power.

Health concerns amongst consumers are increasing and people are much more aware as to how a building can impact wellbeing. Many people suffer from allergies and respiratory difficulties and the right choice of materials is essential in order to reduce the amount of toxic emissions in the building which can cause such illnesses. Baufritz makes regular checks for radioactivity, formaldehyde, chemical wood preservation methods (use of PCP, Lindane) on all its building products and materials to ensure they are not present. The company exclusively uses pollutant-tested, high-quality and environmentally-friendly construction and insulation materials and components.

For example, the choice of insulation material used very much determines the air quality in the building. Baufritz uses its own patented insulation material, Hoiz S45, an insulation material made from wood shavings, sprayed with whey and soda to make them fire, fungus and pesticide resistant. Hoiz S45 is a certified by European building authorities and Natureplus.

In addition, to protect the health of the residents, Baufritz has developed "Xund-E" – a protective shielding concept that is built in to the building's envelope, i.e. external walls and roof, which dramatically reduces the amount of electromagnetic radiation penetrating the home. The Xund-E plate comprises a thin layer of carbon with a layer of natural gypsum, which is then applied to the walls and roofs and then earthed. The board absorbs 99% of high frequency radiation generated from outside the house from sources such as telegraph poles and mobile phone masts. Various studies throughout Europe and the world prove a definitive relation between the increase of cancer and neurological diseases and high frequency radiation and the protection from this harmful influence can also enhance sleep quality for those living in the house. This innovative product is fitted as standard to all Baufritz homes.

Through its own research and collaborations with universities, technical colleges, institutes and the industry itself, Baufritz combines intelligence, competence and experience to develop more truly revolutionary homes that lead the way in terms of health, ecology and building innovation.

Tel: **01223 235632**
Email: **enquiries@baufritz.co.uk**
Website: **www.baufritz.co.uk**

So you're thinking of going green!!

Well, now is the perfect time. Regardless of what inspires your thinking, the conditions are presently positive on all fronts. With houses there are many reasons for going green, some of which are completely altruistic, and some which make very sound economic sense.

Environmental

Whilst the UK has the potential to generate substantial energy from renewable resources, we have to ask ourselves why we aren't taking advantage of these resources and why are we still failing to meet our targets?

With the Kyoto agreement to make a 12.5% reduction in green house gas emissions by 2012, the UK has projected targets doubling our commitment. We still only project an 11% CO_2 reduction, so what does this actually mean? In 1990 green house emissions were 209.5MtC (Million tones of Carbon), 77% percent of this was CO_2.

Economical

Approximately 30% of energy consumption is domestic and an estimated 180,000 new homes are built every year. Each average home uses 4500kWh annually which produces an enormous amount of carbon dioxide, so how can this be reduced?

At Plan-M, we put forward all the options for our clients including solar panels which can supply up to and more than 50% of the average domestic energy requirement. With government grants providing up to 30% of the cost, they're becoming a very effective way of reducing CO_2. Not everyone can take this route but building an energy efficient home or improving an existing dwelling via alternative means is possible for those looking to conserve.

In the end it's about compromise, not everyone wants to discard their cars but implementing effective small changes into the way we develop homes will make a significant overall difference.

This is the time!

S.Maher Director, Plan-M
Website: **www.plan-m.co.uk**   Telephone: **01444 487500**
Email: **admin@plan-m.co.uk**

Plan-M

Bespoke Ecological Homes

From conception to completion,
                  providing a stress free build

Whether you are looking for energy efficient improvements
or a completely self sufficient home,

   our bespoke solutions are tailored to your specifications,
   delivering on budget, on time - every time.

www.plan-m.co.uk   01444 487500   admin@plan-m.co.uk

Ethical purchasing and sourcing

When sourcing materials try to avoid buying items that are harmful or damaging to the environment, and only buy what you need to avoid product and financial waste. Where possible try to use local, natural or renewable sources, and choose durable products that need little maintenance. In some cases you may also be able to obtain salvaged materials from reclamation yards, local refuse sites, skips, charity shops and auction houses (see useful websites below). Only use manufacturers that have a proven environmental management record – they should be able to provide all this information upon request. If they cannot, consider using another company.

If you need to buy timber make sure that it carries the logo of the Forest Stewardship Council (FSC), as this ensures that it has come from responsibly managed forests. Check for rot if reusing old timber, especially dry rot, which smells of mushrooms and has white spreading tendrils. Also, check that the timber has not warped and that it does not contain woodworm, which is characterized by small round holes that may be filled with sawdust if the activity is recent. More information about buying timber is provided in Chapter 9.

When buying materials such as loft insulation, draft proofing, cavity wall insulation and glazing, choose environmentally friendly materials and look for the Energy Saving Recommended logo, as this ensures energy efficiency and will help you to save money on running costs. Contact details of local retailers can be obtained from the Energy Saving Trust website (www.est.org.uk) and green materials and products can be obtained from the Green Building Store (details below).

Generating your own energy

The different types of sustainable energies that are available to homeowners and house-builders are discussed in Chapter 2. If you decide to build your own home you may have more flexibility about the type of energy that you can install, as you can design your house and choose a plot that meets the requirements of your energy source(s). Using your own source of energy also provides the opportunity to build in areas that are not supplied by the national grid, thus cutting down on connection costs and providing more choice about where to build. However, although you will save on connection costs, you must be prepared to spend much more on the installation of renewable energy technologies, although you will make savings on fuel bills over the long term.

If you are considering generating your own energy, the following points will help you to think about the issues involved:

■ Do you need planning permission? Planning issues such as visual impact, noise and conservation will need to be taken into account. The local planning authority will be able to offer advice about whether you need planning permission and whether it is likely to be granted. Certain technologies will not need planning permission, whereas others will, so you should seek specialist advice at the planning and design stage of your project.

■ Are the site conditions suitable for your proposed micro-generation technology? Have these conditions been researched carefully to choose the most appropriate technology? For example, knowledge of local wind conditions is important for designing and positioning wind turbines. To obtain an estimate of wind speeds in the area of your property, consult the UK Wind Speed Database on the British Wind Energy Association website (www.bwea. com).

■ Are you intending to use a stand-alone or a grid-connected system? This will depend on the type of technology that you want to install and the area in which your property is located. If you choose a stand-alone system you may need battery storage, an inverter to convert direct current electricity to alternating current electricity and a controller to divert power to another useful source when the battery is full. You will also need to think about using another energy source, such as a diesel generator when weather conditions are not right for energy generation. If you choose to use a grid-connected system, you still need a converter but no battery storage is required. You can also sell any unused or excess electricity back to your local electricity supply company.

■ What onsite maintenance will be required and how often? Who will carry out this maintenance?

■ What warranties and guarantees are offered on the installation and equipment?

■ What is the expected life-span of turbines, panels and batteries? How often will they have to be replaced and at what cost?

■ How often will equipment need to be serviced?

Obtaining grants and tax incentives

There are a variety of schemes and tax incentives available to people who wish to build their own house in the United Kingdom.

Stamp duty exemption

From April 2007 there will be no stamp duty payable on newly built zero-carbon homes for at least three years. However, some developers and environmentalists are sceptical about the practicalities of such a policy, pointing out that it is unclear how the government is going to measure energy consumption. For example, will this definition relate to the building, the occupants or the construction techniques and materials? At present, there are very few truly zero-carbon buildings in the United Kingdom, and some campaigners believe that there will be such stringent criteria attached to achieving exemption that it will be impossible for builders and developers to obtain. If you are hoping to build a zero-carbon home you will need to seek specialist advice at the planning and design stage. More information can be obtained from the AECB (details below) and from the Green Building website: www.newbuilder.co.uk.

DIY builders and converters refund scheme

If you are intending to build your own property, it is possible to claim a VAT refund on your main construction costs. However, you are excluded under this scheme if your development is for business purposes, such as speculative development or to let to tenants. Rules and regulations are complex and you should seek further advice if you wish to take advantage of this scheme. It is possible to hire a VAT consultant to make a refund claim for you. More information about hiring a consultant can be obtained from the Institute of Indirect Taxation (www.theiit.org.uk).

The Scottish Community and Householder Renewables Initiative

If you are a builder, developer or architect living in Scotland it is possible to apply for grants for renewable energy technologies on behalf of future owners of houses you are building or designing through the Scottish Community and Householder Renewables Initiative (see the Appendix).

Low Carbon Buildings Programme

Through the Low Carbon Buildings Programme individual householders can apply for grants to help with the installation of renewable sources of energy for their homes. This includes new-build and covers the installation of solar photovoltaics, wind turbines, small hydro, solar thermal hot water, heat pumps (ground/water/air source) and bio-energy. More information about these grants can be obtained from the DTI's Low Carbon Buildings Programme website (www.lowcarbonbuildings.org.uk) or by telephoning 0800 915 0990.

Summary

Self-build provides a good opportunity to plan and design a house that suits your wants, needs and green requirements. However, choosing this option requires a great deal of research, hard work, commitment, patience and enough up-front finance to be able to begin, and see through, the project. Nevertheless, once you have built your eco-home the personal, financial and environmental rewards will be worth all the time and effort that have gone into the construction of your home.

The final phase of your new-build project will involve landscaping and gardening, and again, there are many ways that your garden design and gardening habits can reflect your green philosophy. These issues are discussed in the following chapter.

Useful organizations

Royal Institute of Chartered Surveyors (RICS)

The RICS is the largest organization for professionals working in property, land and construction worldwide. RICS members have to adhere to a strict code of conduct and are required to update their skills and knowledge continually. All members must have proper insurance and customers are protected by an RICS formal complaints service.

Royal Institute of Chartered Surveyors
RICS Contact Centre
Surveyor Court, Westwood Way
Coventry CV4 8JE
Tel: 0870 333 1600
Fax: 020 7334 3811
E-mail: contactrics@rics.org
Website: www.rics.org

Planning Inspectorate

The Planning Inspectorate processes planning and enforcement appeals, and holds inquiries into local development plans in England and Wales.

Planning Inspectorate
Temple Quay House, 2 The Square
Bristol BS1 6PN
Tel: 0117 372 6372
Fax: 0117 372 8443
E-mail: enquiries@planning-pins.gsi.gov.uk
Website: www.planning-inspectorate.gov.uk

Royal Institute of British Architects (RIBA)

RIBA is a member organization with over 30,000 members worldwide. You can find an architect using one of the online directories.

Royal Institute of British Architects
RIBA Client Services
66 Portland Place
London W1B 1AD
Tel: 020 7580 5533
Fax: 020 7255 1541
E-mail: info@inst.riba.org
Website: www.riba.org

Straw Bale Building Association (SBBA)

SBBA is an informal association of people who have an interest in straw bale building. Members include environmental enthusiasts, sustainable builders, architects and building officials. The SBBA offers courses, workshops, books and videos for anyone interested in straw bale information.

Straw Bale Building Association
Hollinroyd Farm, Butts Lane
Todmorden OL14 8RJ
Tel: 01442 825 421
E-mail: info@stawbalebuildingassociation.org.uk
Website: www.srawbalebuildingassociation.org.uk

UK Timber Frame Association

The UK Timber Frame Association is the trade association for UK timber frame manufacturers, and the sector's key supplier. You can find a timber frame manufacturer, designer, erector and supplier on the website, along with useful information about all aspects of the timber frame construction method.

UK Timber Frame Association
The e-centre
Cooperage Way Business Village
Alloa FK10 3LP
Tel: 01259 272140
Fax: 01259 272141
E-mail: office@timber-frame.org
Website: www.timber-frame.org

WWF

WWF is the world's largest independent conservation charity, and was established in the United Kingdom in 1961. WWF-UK is involved in the 'One Million Sustainable Homes' project, which involves working with government, industry and consumers to bring sustainable homes from the fringes of the housing sector to the mainstream. On its website you can download an information leaflet to find out more about this project. You can also access the 'housebuilder sustainability toolkit', which offers advice on sustainability issues to house-builders.

WWF-UK
Panda House, Weyside Park
Godalming
Surrey, GU7 1XR
Tel: 01483 426444
Fax: 01483 426409
www.wwf.org.uk
E-mail: england@wwf.org.uk

Building Research Establishment (BRE)

BRE is a collection of research scientists, engineers, architects, surveyors, psychologists, administrators, managers and others who bring together their knowledge and expertise to advise on sustainable construction and the built environment. They provide a variety of consultancy, testing and commissioned research services. The BRE bookshop provides a full range of sustainable construction books.

Building Research Establishment Ltd
Bucknalls Lane
Watford WD25 9XX
Tel: 01923 664 000
E-mail: enquiries@bre.co.uk
Website: www.bre.co.uk

Useful websites

www.planningportal.gov.uk
On this website you can find detailed information about planning permission and building regulations, including details of your local planning authority and local development plans. The website guides you through the planning process, providing comprehensive and user-friendly information and advice for anyone wishing to make a planning application. Depending on where you intend to build, you may be able to make an application online once you have registered.

www.plotfinder.net
This is a subscription service for providing building plots and renovation projects in the United Kingdom, in association with *Homebuilding and Renovating* magazine.

www.propertyspy.com
This company offers land for sale on greenfield and green-belt sites around the United Kingdom. However, the land purchase is speculative – no planning permission is offered on the plots.

www.plotbrowser.com
This website is a subscription service in conjunction with *Selfbuild and Design* magazine, offering regularly updated information about plots, conversion or renovation opportunities in the United Kingdom.

www.self-build.co.uk
This website provides useful information about all aspects of self-build, including mortgages, insurance, warranties, finding suppliers and manufacturers, and finding land.

www.buildstore.co.uk
This website provides useful information about all aspects of self-build, including useful measurement converters, advice about house design, sourcing materials, building regulations, construction costs, planning considerations and obtaining value for money.

www.aecb.net
The Association for Environment Conscious Building (AECB) is a network of individuals and companies with a common aim of promoting sustainable building. On the website you can find information about improving the environmental performance of your property; choosing eco-friendly products and avoiding damaging chemicals; using timber; and planning and developing eco-friendly properties. The message-board service is a useful way to receive tailor-made advice and information about all aspects of self-build.

www.salvoweb.com
Salvo is a partnership that aims to support dealers who hold stocks of architectural salvage, reclaimed building materials, demolition salvage and recycled materials. Where possible it encourages fair

trade and eco-friendly activities. Contact details for dealers, suppliers and craftspeople can be obtained from the website.

Further reading

Chiras, D (2004) *The New Ecological Home: A complete guide to green building options*, Chelsea Green, Post Mills, Vermont

Dean, A (2003) *Green by Design*, Gibbs M Smith, Layton, Utah

Hall, K (ed) (2005) *The Green Building Bible*, Green Building Press, Llandysul

Harris, C and Borer, P (2005) *The Whole House Book: Ecological building design and materials*, 2nd edn, Centre for Alternative Technology, Machynlleth

Kennedy, J et al (2002) *The Art of Natural Building: Design, construction, resources*, New Society, Gabriola Island, British Colombia

Roaf, S (2001) *Eco House: A design guide*, Architectural Press, Oxford

Snell, C and Callahan, T (2005) *Building Green: A complete how-to guide to alternative building methods*, Lark Books, Asheville, North Carolina

Vale, B and Vale, R (2002) *The New Autonomous House: Design and planning for sustainability*, Thames and Hudson, London

11 Gardeners

Making changes to your gardening habits is one of the easiest ways to work towards achieving your green goals. Even if you do not have a large garden it is possible to make significant changes that can help you to save money while improving the health of your family and helping the environment.

This chapter offers advice on reusing and recycling, composting, organic growing, conserving water and energy in the garden, sourcing environmentally friendly products and finding out about grants and discount schemes.

Reusing and recycling

Gardens provide an ideal opportunity to reuse and recycle waste from the home and from the garden. Both garden and household waste can be composted and reused on the garden, although care needs to be taken when deciding what materials can be composted (see below). Other items from the house can be reused in the garden, such as plastic bottles to help direct water to plant roots and keep slugs and snails and bad weather from young plants; old carpets to cover compost heaps; used ground coffee laid around favourite plants to deter slugs and snails; old pots, pans and other containers used for planting or rainwater collection. Also, use recycled materials when designing your garden: for example you can use 'glass' gravel instead of freshly mined rock, and starter plant pots made from recycled newspapers. To find a company offering recycled products for your garden, consult the Recycled Products Guide (www.recycledproducts.org.uk).

If you do not compost your own garden waste you should take advantage of the green waste disposal service run by your local authority. This green waste is composted and offered back to local residents, usually free of charge or for a small fee. This means that care should be taken to ensure that the waste is not contaminated with products that cannot be composted, such as plastics or wood that has been treated with preservatives. Also, you should not include paper, cardboard or kitchen waste with your green waste. Some local authorities place restrictions on the amount of compost you can take each visit if it is free, and you will need to provide your own bags and shovel. This is a useful source of soil improver for people who are unable to compost their own material. Contact your local authority for details about green waste disposal schemes in your area.

Composting

Composting is an excellent form of recycling. It is a useful way to get rid of garden and kitchen waste, and when dug into the garden, compost provides valuable nutrients and improves the structure of your soil. It is not necessary to buy an expensive compost bin, unless you wish to do so for aesthetic reasons. Instead you can make your own compost heap in a corner of your garden, or obtain a cheap or free compost bin from your local authority (see below). If you want your composting to work quickly, your bin or heap should be at least a metre cubed in size.

When building your heap or placing your bin, do so on a piece of strong wire mesh as this will discourage rodents. You can compost anything that has lived, but you should avoid fish and meat bones as, again, this will help to discourage rodents. It is also better to avoid perennial weeds and diseased plants – the heat of the tip may kill some, but not all, diseases and weeds. You should compost both green material (soft garden waste such as grass) and brown material (straw, hay and twigs) at a ratio of about 25:1. Sawdust and wood shavings can be used sparingly, but make sure that they have not been treated with wood preserver. Tough items will need to be chopped with shears before composting. Glossy paper and colour print should be avoided.

A good way to start the bin is to use grass cuttings interspersed with layers of crumpled newspaper to a depth of at least 30 centimetres, covering with a layer of old carpet, or a lid, to keep the rain out. The compost needs to be kept moist but not too wet, or it will begin to smell strongly and will not rot down as quickly. You may need to add water if your compost is too dry. The contents of the bin should be moved around or stirred up once the temperature begins to fall.

In the summer it should take six to eight weeks for the heap to finish composting, and in this time it will need stirring two or three times. Through the colder months, or in colder climates, a heap can take up to a year to finish. In general, the more effort you put into managing your compost, the quicker it will finish.

More information about composting can be obtained from some of the publications listed below or from the Garden Organic website (details below). The Community Composting Network supports and promotes the community management and use of waste biodegradable resources, and offers advice and training on all aspects of community composting (www.communitycompost.org).

Worm composting

If you have children they might be interested in worm composting. This is an environmentally friendly activity that can take place all year long with minimum effort and knowledge. The worms are native red worms, which differ from earthworms in that they live on decaying organic matter rather than in the soil. However, if the worms escape they will not do any damage to your garden.

Worms digest waste to produce worm castings, and unlike other composting methods, wormeries do not work at high temperatures. In general, if you start a wormery with around 1,000 worms, your compost will be ready to use on the garden in 8 to 12 months. The worms are able to digest cooked and uncooked fruit and vegetable waste, stale bread, tea bags and eggshells. They can also eat some paper and cardboard in small amounts and coffee grounds in small amounts. You should avoid glass, treated woods, metals, meat scraps and dairy products.

Some of the websites listed below supply wormeries and offer more information about their use, or contact your local authority to find out whether it offers subsidized wormeries. More information about using wormeries can be obtained from the RHS website (details below).

Organic growing

Traditional agricultural systems controlled pests and disease through diversification and crop rotation, with farmers planting a wide variety of crops alongside each other and changing crops on a regular basis. This slowed the spread of disease and pests that are common in today's intensive, chemically dependent agricultural production, where one commercial crop dominates and chemical companies influence what farmers use on their land.

Today there are several hundred pesticide chemicals that are used in intensive food production around the world, both to grow and store the crop. The problems associated with such widespread use of pesticides do not only involve the risk of consuming materials that may be harmful to our health, but also include the exposure of agricultural workers to pesticides, exposure to local inhabitants and environmental damage. The Pesticide Action Network UK (PAN UK) points out that, at present, the UK government only tests for a proportion of these chemicals, and since it is impossible to tell through taste and smell what we are consuming, we do not know what we are ingesting and what harm is being caused. These problems can be reduced through direct action such as lobbying politicians and supermarkets, by buying organic, ethical or Fairtrade produce or through growing your own fruit and vegetables. For more information about all these issues, consult the websites of Fairtrade, PAN UK or the Ethical Trading Initiative (details below).

Biological and natural pest control

If you decide to grow your own produce, or want to discourage pests from other plants, there are many ways that you can do so without resorting to the use of harmful chemicals:

- Understand the enemy. Get to know more about the pests that are attacking your plants. Once you know more about the pests you can find out how to deter them from your garden. Consult the RHS website for information and advice about common pests and diseases (details below).

- There are many plants that different pests don't like, and these can be planted in among other plants to deter pests. For example, it is thought that slugs hate aromatic plants such as lavender and chives, while rosemary and sage may deter carrot fly.

- Create a wildlife garden that encourages natural predators such as toads, frogs, hedgehogs and ladybirds (see below).

- Use humane traps and solar-powered electronic deterrents to discourage pests such as mice and cockroaches. Beer traps or upturned flowerpots can be used to catch slugs and snails.

▊ Some pests, such as carrot fly, only create problems up to a certain height from the ground, so utilize raised planters or surround your crops with lightweight screens to stop the problem.

▊ Reduce moist, shady areas in the garden that encourage snails and slugs. Thin out plants and encourage air to circulate.

▊ Lay thick layers of mulch on open areas to discourage snails and slugs. They tend to dislike materials with rough and jagged edges.

▊ Use decoys to discourage pests from favourite plants. For example you can use a barrier of vegetation such as comfrey leaves, which tend to be favoured by slugs.

▊ Use barriers to deter pests: for example, wood ash or pure coal soot will discourage slugs.

▊ Hand pick slugs and snails from your garden. Although this can be time-consuming, it is a very effective control method. The best time is two hours after sunset, and you should search for the pests in moist areas and on the underside of leaves.

Soil management

Soil management is an important part of organic growing. Through careful management you can help to enhance soil drainage, improve soil structure, boost fertility and prevent drought stress, no matter what your soil type. Soil is made up of water, minerals, air and organic matter. Within the soil there are a wide variety of living organisms such as earthworms, fungi, bacteria, protozoa, arthropods and algae. Soil organic matter contains dead organisms, plant matter and other organic matter at various stages of decomposition. Organic matter serves as a reservoir for plant nutrients and helps to build soil structure and improve texture. For an organic grower it is important to maintain a balanced soil composition and encourage living organisms that will help to improve the quality of the soil.

One of the easiest ways to do this is through composting (see above). If you do not have your own compost and you need to buy some, make sure that the Soil Association symbol is on the bag, as this ensures that the material is organic (details below). Other compost can be obtained from your local waste and recycling centre.

Another way to improve the quality of your soil is to double-dig it in the autumn, as frost will help to break it down further. When the bed is dug for the first time you will need to add plenty of organic matter and break down the clods as much as possible. If you are applying leaf mould or manure for food crops, do so in the spring before you begin to grow your plants. Try to limit the amount of walking on freshly dug soil as it will begin to compact. Keep soil surfaces covered at all times, using old carpet or mulch in the winter, compost in the spring and crop cover in the summer and autumn. This will keep weeds down, retain water and prevent problems with erosion, leaching and compaction.

As an organic grower you should not use any products that will harm the soil or the living organisms within the soil, such as weed killers or slug pellets. Use the biological control methods described above to control pests and disease. For more information about soil management contact the RHS or HYDRA (details below).

Growing food

For first-time growers it is important to discuss what to grow with all members of the family – adults and children are more likely to become involved and help with the workload if they like what they are going to eat. It is also useful to plan your garden and conduct careful research into which type of plants grow in the best locations. You need to find out what food grows at what time of the year, and plan your garden so that you have food all year round. Some crops have a specific harvest time – stagger planting so that you are not inundated with too much of one crop at one time. If you have a small garden, grow food that only needs a small space and avoid spreading plants. Avoid planting under trees or in areas that have too much shade or little natural water. You should try to avoid planting against large north-facing walls, as these have little sunlight and create a rain shadow.

Try to use organically grown seeds where possible and find out whether it is possible to source seeds and plants locally, as this will help you to understand what local varieties will suit the conditions in your garden. Avoid genetically modified varieties, and avoid the use of slug pellets and weed killers (see above). On the Garden Organic website there is a large amount of useful information about growing organic food, including ideas about the varieties of plants to use, recognizing and dealing with weeds, and treating common diseases without the use of toxic chemicals (details below).

Creating a wildlife garden

Creating a wildlife garden is an enjoyable and educational activity for children, and it encourages natural predators that will help to control the pests in your garden. When creating your garden you need to think about four things to encourage wildlife – food, water, shelter and places to breed. Also, if you add plenty of variety to the structure and design of your garden, you will increase the number of wildlife visitors throughout the year. Trees, bird boxes and feeders encourage birds, and hedges are more effective at encouraging wildlife than fences. If you are unable to grow a hedge, use trellis to grow climbing plants up walls and fences.

When planting, choose trees and shrubs that provide berries for birds and other creatures, and try to ensure that plants flower at different times of the year to encourage bees and other insects over a longer period. Useful information about native and non-native trees, shrubs and hedges can be obtained from the Wild about Gardens website (details below).

Ponds will encourage frogs and toads, especially if they have a marshy area to provide shelter for their young. When creating a pond, make sure that the edges are not too steep. Instead they should be gently sloping so that amphibians and other creatures, such as hedgehogs, can climb out. The centre of the pond needs to be deep enough that it does not freeze in winter – around 55–70 centimetres will probably be enough. If you are filling the pond with tap water, let it rest for a few days so that the chlorine can dissipate and then add a bucket of water from a mature pond. This will contain plant spores and cells that will help to colonize your pond. Bird baths or small fountains provide water for bathing and drinking when a pond is not practical. For more information about creating a wildlife pond, consult the Pond Conservation Trust website (www.pondtrust.org.uk).

Conserving water and energy

As our climate becomes more unpredictable and droughts more common, it is important to think about ways of conserving water in the garden. There are many simple, cheap and effective changes that can be made with only a small amount of effort on your part:

■ Save water in the garden by making sure that your soil is rich in organic matter (see above).

■ If you are very serious about saving water you could think about installing rainwater harvesting systems or a gravity-fed system for toilets. These types of system would need the backing of the whole family, and you should carefully compare the costs with the environmental benefits. More information about rainwater harvesting systems can be obtained from the UK Rainwater Harvesting Association (details below).

■ During hosepipe bans, remove half the leaves of large-leafed plants and water as close to the roots as possible. A funnel or half a bottle dug into the soil directly over the roots will help you to target the water and reduce wastage. Consult the RHS website for up-to-date information about which areas in the country are experiencing a hosepipe ban (details below).

■ Cover the soil with mulch to retain water, especially over the drier summer months. You can recycle household materials for this purpose.

■ Use as many water butts as the size of your property and garden will allow. Collect rainwater from the roof of your home, sheds, greenhouses and garages. Suitable water butts can be ordered from the CAT website (www.cat.org.uk/shopping).

■ Recycle 'greywater' from the home, including the bath, shower and kitchen sink. However, make sure that you have not used strong detergents and that the water is not too salty or greasy, and spread the water thinly across a large area. Soaps and shampoos in the water will not harm your plants. Simple diversion kits are available to help you divert water from your downpipe into butts (see websites below).

■ Use drip or trickle irrigation systems, rather than hosepipes or sprinklers.

■ Buy and plant new plants in autumn and spring so that they get more rainwater and need less watering.

■ Pots, containers and hanging baskets need more watering, so keep their use to a minimum.

■ Dig soil in the autumn and never in the summer, as much water can be lost through evaporation.

▌ Choose drought-resistant plants. Advice about these plants is offered on the RHS website (details below).

Conserving energy in the garden is also important, and today there are a number of products that utilize solar power, including solar-powered garden lights, solar water pumps and solar water fountains for garden water features, and electronic deterrent devises for pests, which also run on solar power. These products are available from good garden centres or from some of the online shops listed below.

Sourcing environmentally friendly products and materials

There are a variety of companies that specialize in providing products for gardeners who are interested in environmentally friendly products and materials (see useful websites below). *The Organic Directory* is a useful book that lists certified organic vegetable box schemes, shops, restaurants and other useful information (details below). To check the green credentials of produce or products look for endorsement and/or support from any of the following organizations:

▌ the Wildlife Trust;

▌ the Birdcare Standards Association;

▌ the British Trust for Ornithology;

▌ the Royal Society for the Protection of Birds;

▌ the Royal Society for the Prevention of Cruelty to Animals;

▌ the World Wildlife Fund;

▌ the Birds and Business Alliance;

▌ the Vegetarian Society;

▌ the Barn Owl Trust;

▌ the Royal Horticultural Society;

▌ Butterfly Conservation;

▌ English Nature;

▌ the Mammals Trust;

■ the Woodland Trust;

■ the Ponds Conservation Trust;

■ the Soil Association.

Certification

There are a number of organizations that certify organic produce and products sold in the United Kingdom. Traders should display a certificate and have a trading schedule that lists all the products that have been licensed by the relevant organization. If you are in doubt about the organic credentials of produce or products, you should ask to see the certificate or the trading schedule. If the trader is unable to produce this, yet is selling the produce as organic, it is recommended that you report him or her to the relevant certifying body or to your local trading standards office. Certification bodies for which you can check include:

■ The Soil Association (www.soilassociation.org);

■ Organic Farmers and Growers Limited (www.organicfarmers. com);

■ the Scottish Organic Producers Association (www.sopa.org.uk);

■ the Organic Food Federation (www.orgfoodfed.com);

■ Demeter (the Biodynamic Agricultural Association: www.bio dynamic.org.uk);

■ the Irish Organic Farmers and Growers Association (www. irishorganic.ie);

■ Organic Trust Ltd (www.organic-trust.org);

■ CMi Certification (www.cmi-plc.com);

■ Quality Welsh Food Certification (www.wfsagri.net);

■ Ascisco Limited (www.soilassociation.org).

Knowing about grants and discount schemes

Many local authorities have a scheme through which they provide compost bins at a greatly reduced price or free of charge. Contact your local authority for information about your local scheme. You can also contact your local authority for details of its Local Agenda 21 plan. These plans came about as a result of the 1992 Earth Summit in Rio de Janeiro, at which the Agenda 21 plan was devised as a way to move towards sustainable development. Local authorities were asked to devise a plan that would protect the local environment, use local resources and services, and use natural resources more efficiently. Through this plan local authorities offer grants to local communities to improve the environment in which they live. Examples of schemes include the Environment and Countryside Grant Scheme and the Biodiversity Grant Scheme. Contact your local authority to find out what grants are available, and for information about eligibility criteria.

Although funding organizations are unlikely to offer grants to individuals for creating a more environmentally friendly garden for personal use, there are a number of other organizations that will offer money to community groups for various types of green project, including creating an organic garden for community use, or for cleaning and tidying derelict land. For more information about grants, application procedures and eligibility criteria, contact the relevant organization:

■ Awards for all (tel: 0845 600 2040; website: www.awardsforall. org.uk);

■ Big Lottery Fund (tel: 0845 410 2030; website: www.biglotteryfund. org.uk);

■ Heritage Lottery Fund (tel: 0207 591 6042; website: www.hlf.org. uk);

■ Lottery Funding (tel: 0845 275 0000; website: www.lotteryfunding. org.uk).

Summary

There are many environmentally friendly changes that you can make in your garden, including reusing and recycling household materials and organic matter, composting, organic cultivation, creating a wildlife garden, buying environmentally friendly products, and conserving water and energy. Most of these changes are cheap to make, some will save you money, and with a little time and effort you will have a good supply of free food.

Throughout the book advice and information has been offered on all aspects of buying, developing and investing in green property. As with gardening discussed in this chapter, many of the changes you make will lead to financial savings, a healthier lifestyle and help to improve the environment for future generations. Useful addresses and websites are provided at the end of the book for those of you who wish to carry out further research. I wish you every success in achieving your green property goals.

Useful organizations

The Royal Horticultural Society (RHS)

The RHS is a UK charity dedicated to advancing horticulture and promoting good gardening. You can obtain information and advice about all aspects of horticulture from the RHS. The website contains a useful problem solver that helps you to understand and solve problems you may face in your garden, such as pests, plant disease and fungi.

Royal Horticultural Society
80 Vincent Square
London SW1P 2PE
Tel: 0845 260 5000
E-mail: info@rhs.org.uk
Website: www.rhs.org.uk

The Wildlife Trust

The Wildlife Trust is a partnership of 47 wildlife trusts across the United Kingdom. It is a UK charity dedicated to conserving wildlife habitats and species. You can find out more about its work, obtain useful publications and find information about your local trust on the website.

The Wildlife Trust
The Kiln, Waterside, Mather Road
Newark
Nottinghamshire NG24 1WT
Tel: 0870 036 7711

Fax: 0870 036 0101
E-mail: enquiry@wildlifetrusts.org
Website: www.wildlifetrusts.org

Garden Organic

Garden Organic is the working name of the Henry Doubleday
Research Association (HDRA), which is a charity for organic growing,
dedicated to helping gardeners, farmers and members of the public
who are interested in organic methods. On its website you can find
useful information about all aspects of organic growing, including
composting, sourcing products, school projects and obtaining
organic food on a budget.

Garden Organic
Ryton Organic Gardens
Coventry
Warwickshire CV8 3LG
Tel: 024 7630 3517
Fax: 024 7663 9229
E-mail: enquiry@hydra.org.uk
Website: www.gardenorganic.org.uk

The Soil Association

The Soil Association is an environmental charity that promotes
sustainable, organic farming. Through Soil Association Certification
Ltd, organic certification is offered to farmers, growers, food processors and packers, retailers, caterers, textile producers, health and
beauty manufacturers and importers from the United Kingdom and
overseas. You can look for this certification when checking to see
that the products you are buying are organic. The Soil Association
website contains useful information on living an organic lifestyle.

The Soil Association
Bristol House, 40–56 Victoria Street
Bristol BS1 6BY
Tel: 0117 314 5000
Fax: 0117 314 5001
E-mail: info@soilassociation.org
Website: www.soilassociation.org

Pesticide Action Network UK (PAN UK)

PAN UK is an independent, non-profit organization that promotes healthy food, agriculture and an environment that will provide food and meet public health needs without dependence on toxic chemicals, and without harm to food producers and agricultural workers. On its website you can find useful information and publications on a wide variety of issues concerning the avoidance of toxic chemicals, controlling pests in the garden and home, and disposing safely of unwanted pesticides.

Pesticide Action Network UK
Development House
56–64 Leonard Street
London EC2A 4JH
Tel: 020 7065 0905
Fax: 020 7064 0907
E-mail: admin@pan-uk.org
Website: www.pan-uk.org

The Fairtrade Foundation

The Fairtrade Foundation licenses the FAIRTRADE mark to products in the United Kingdom that meet international fair trade standards. This mark is an independent consumer label that appears on products as a guarantee that disadvantaged producers in the developing world are getting a better deal. You can find out more about Fairtrade products and suppliers on its website.

The Fairtrade Foundation
Room 204, 16 Baldwin's Gardens
London EC1N 7RJ
Tel: 020 7405 5942
Fax: 020 7405 5943
E-mail: mail@fairtrade.org.uk
Website: www.fairtrade.org.uk

The Ethical Trading Initiative (ETI)

ETI is an alliance of companies, NGOs and trade union organizations. It exists to ensure that the working conditions of workers producing for the UK market meet or exceed international labour standards. On the website you can find more information about ethical trade.

The Ethical Trading Initiative
2nd floor, Cromwell House
14 Fulwood Place
London WC1V 6HZ
Tel: 020 7404 1463
Fax: 020 7831 7852
E-mail: eti@eti.org.uk
Website: www.ethicaltrade.org.uk

Useful websites

www.wildaboutgardens.org
This is a new project from the RHS and Wildlife Trusts that aims to bring together the worlds of gardening and nature conservation for the benefit of people and wildlife. On the website you can find useful information and advice about establishing a wildlife garden.

www.ukrha.org
The UK Rainwater Harvesting Association (UK-RHA) is a company limited by guarantee that serves to act as a focal point for organizations with business interests in the rainwater harvesting industry. On its website you can access more information about rainwater harvesting and obtain contact details of members.

www.ernest-charles.com
This is the website of Earnest Charles, a company that specializes in products for garden wildlife, including safe and humane deterrents for pests, soil improvers, bird seed, feeders and baths, books and gifts. The company helps to develop bird feed products and contributes to wildlife trusts. More information and the online store can be accessed from the website.

www.naturalgardening.co.uk
On this website you will find a range of fertilizers and compost balancers that will help you to enrich your garden soil in an organic way.

www.impactpublishing.co.uk
Impact Publishing specializes in modern, practical guides to gardening, lifestyle choices and the environment. On its website you can find books about creating wildlife gardens and ponds, green parenting, growing fruit and vegetables and producing perfect lawns.

www.greenpestco.com
The Green Pest Company is a family-run business that supplies environmentally friendly products to control pests.

www.recycleworks.co.uk
This company manufactures and sells recycling products such as composting equipment, water butts, waste organization systems and shredders. It also has a 'giveaway' service that enables users to offer unwanted items in good condition free of charge.

www.wigglywigglers.co.uk
This company offers sustainable products that offer value for money, from various type of worm composting equipment to bird boxes and feeders. On the website you can find useful advice about worm composting.

Further reading

Litchfield, C (ed) (2005) *The Organic Directory 2006*, Green Books, Totnes
Roulac, J (1998) *Backyard Composting*, Green Books, Totnes
Scott, N (2003) *Composting for All*, Green Books, Totnes
Warren, P (2003) *How to Store your Garden Produce: The key to self sufficiency*, Green Books, Totnes

Appendix
Grants, loans and tax incentives

Regional schemes

Local authorities throughout the United Kingdom offer a number of grants for homeowners and landlords to improve their property. In most cases, homeowners will need to be in receipt of state benefits, classed as 'vulnerable' homeowners or on low incomes. Those who are on low incomes must complete a 'financial resources' form which provides information about their personal income, and this must be backed up with evidence. Grants for landlords tend not to be means-tested. Instead, a landlord may receive a percentage of the cost of the work, rather than the full amount that would be payable to means-tested homeowners.

Eligibility criteria vary between local authorities, and will depend on the grant for which you are applying. However, for homeowner grants you will need to hold the freehold of the property, intend to live in the property for a specified number of years and have the property as your sole residence. You will also need to meet the financial criteria mentioned above. Landlords will need to demonstrate that they intend to let the property for a specified number of years after improvements have been made.

Application procedures vary, but in general you will need to check that you meet the eligibility criteria, fill in the appropriate forms, including a financial assessment, and provide the required evidence. This could include bank statements, wage slips and benefit books. Your local authority will let you know whether your application has been successful, and if not, will tell you why. In most cases you have the right to appeal against the decision. In some local authorities, even if your application is successful, you will be placed on a waiting list until funds become available.

In some cases an environmental health officer or improvement grants officer will visit your property to assess your needs and help you to find out which grants are the most suitable. A schedule of works will be drawn up to itemize the work that needs doing.

Some local authorities have a list of approved contractors that must be used to carry out the work, whereas others require you to obtain quotations from local contractors. If this is the case, the local authority will inspect the quotation to check that it is reasonable, and will want contact details for the contractor, to check that he or she is legitimate and not a relation or friend of yours. Some will provide a list of builders to help you choose a reliable organization

Local authority schemes vary from year to year, depending on the funds available, so contact the housing section of your local authority to find out what is available. Many now publish details of their grants on their website or publish an information leaflet on 'housing grants' or 'energy-efficiency grants'. The following grants are examples of what may be available in your region.

Home energy efficiency grants

These grants are available to help owner-occupiers, landlords and tenants to install energy-efficient heating and insulation. The grants are means-tested and available to homeowners and tenants who are on means-tested benefits or low incomes. Landlords are not means-tested, but only receive a percentage of the cost of works. Schemes vary between local authorities and depend upon available funds. If funds are not available applicants are placed on a waiting list. Schemes should cover some or all of the following energy efficient improvements:

- wall insulation;
- loft insulation;
- lagging of pipes and cylinders;
- draft proofing of windows and doors;
- energy-efficient lighting;
- heating controls including timer, hot water thermostat and thermostatic radiator valves;

- a central heating system with condensing boiler where there is no central heating system installed;
- additional ventilation where required.

Energy grants

Some local authorities offer grants to homeowners or tenants who do not qualify for the type of grants mentioned above or for the Warm Front scheme mentioned below. The grants are available for various types of insulation and removal of old materials. The schemes are administered by home improvement agencies (HIA), and specific eligibility criteria apply, so you should contact your local HIA for more information (see Chapter 1).

Renovation grants

Renovation grants are designed to help owner-occupiers carry out repairs or improvements to their properties. However, in some areas the grants are available for tenants, if they have a full repairing lease or a fixed-term tenancy of at least five years, and for landlords. Some local authorities enable you to include energy-efficiency improvements in the works.

In most cases these grants are discretionary and will depend on the funds available. To obtain a grant you will need to hold the freehold and intend to live or let the property for a specified number of years. Your property will need to have been classed 'unfit' for habitation or failed the new Housing Health and Safety Rating System (HHSRS) assessment. This came into force in April 2006 in England and later in the year in Wales. It is a new risk assessment tool used to assess potential risks to the health and safety of occupants in residential properties, and it replaces the Housing Fitness Standard which was set out in the Housing Act 1985. You will not be eligible for a grant if the work can be carried out under other assistance such as an insurance or third-party claim. The grant is means-tested.

Empty property grants

These grants are available to help people interested in restoring an empty property. Local authorities will pay a percentage of the cost of works, usually in the region of 30–70 per cent, with most specifying an upper cost limit, usually around £10,000. The amount of grant you will receive depends on a number of factors, including the type and size of property, its location and the intended use once the work is complete. If you sell the property within a specified number of years you will have to repay the grant.

Some local authorities specify the amount of time that a property must have been empty before a grant will be offered, and some will only offer grants if the property is to be made available for private letting through a registered social landlord. If this is the case, local authorities are very specific about the end product, in terms of size of rooms, standard of accommodation, décor, fixtures and fittings, energy efficiency and heating. Once the property is renovated it must meet the criteria set out in the new HHSRS. If you cease to let the property within a specified period of time, you will have to repay the grant.

Loan scheme for housing repairs

Some local authorities offer loans to homeowners and landlords who wish to repair and renovate their property. In some cases loans will only be given if the property has been deemed unfit for human habitation. The loans are interest free and repayable by homeowners either when the property is sold or bequeathed, or in the case of landlords, after five years. Local authorities specify a maximum amount of loan, which could be up to £20,000, and need to approve a schedule of works before a loan will be granted.

Homeowners should check that this is the most suitable method of raising finances, as, in the event of their death, relatives will need to pay back the loan, whether or not they sell the property.

Houses in multiple occupation (HMO) grants

A house in multiple occupation (HMO) is defined as 'a house which is occupied by persons who do not form a single household'. Local authorities offer discretionary grants to landlords to help them make an HMO fit for human habitation, or carry out repairs or upgrade for the number of occupiers. This includes grants to improve energy efficiency.

Some local authorities place a limit on the amount of grant available, whereas others do not have a maximum limit, but the number of grants available is restricted by available finances. In most cases landlords must make a means-tested contribution towards the works, based on the rent to be received from the property. Grants are not given until the required planning permissions and building regulations approval have been granted.

The property will need to continue to be let for a specified period, must be adequately insured and must be maintained in a fit condition. Some local authorities specify the rent levels that must be charged, and require the grant to be repaid in full if conditions are breached or the property is sold within a specified period.

National schemes

There are a number of schemes that are available for homeowners, landlords and and/or developers across one or more countries of the United Kingdom, as described below.

The Home Energy Efficiency Scheme (Wales)

This scheme is available for homeowners and tenants who live in Wales. It is aimed primarily at households with the greatest health risks – older people, people with children under the age of 16 and people who are disabled and chronically sick. Through this scheme a grant of up to £2,700 is provided to make homes warmer, more energy efficient and more secure. The grant can be used for the following improvements:

- loft insulation;
- cavity wall insulation;
- draught-proofing;
- hot water tank insulation;
- gas room heaters with thermostatic controls;
- electric storage heaters;
- converting a solid-fuel open fire to a modern glass-fronted fire;
- low-energy light bulbs.

When an enquiry is received, an approved surveyor is sent to your property to make an assessment and decide upon the most appropriate improvements, explain the scheme and help you to fill in the relevant forms. An approved contractor is arranged to carry out the work. The scheme is funded by the National Assembly for Wales and managed by the Eaga Group (see useful organizations). More information about the scheme can be obtained by telephoning 0800 316 2815.

Warm Front (England)

Warm Front was launched in June 2000 as the Home Energy Efficiency Scheme. Through this scheme a grant of £2,700 or £4,000 (if oil central heating has been recommended) is available to certain households in England. To qualify for the scheme you must own your own home or rent from a private landlord, have a child under 16 or be at least 26 weeks pregnant, and be in receipt of state benefits.

An assessor will visit your home to decide what energy efficiency measures need to put into place. If the cost of these measures exceeds the total value of the grant, householders may be required to make a contribution. The scheme manager appoints an approved contractor to carry out the work (see Eaga Group in useful organizations).

If you are a private landlord you will need to agree to all the works and may need to pay an additional contribution. Once the work has been carried out you are not able to increase the rent on your property until one year after insulation measures have been installed and two years after heating measures have been installed. More information about the scheme can be obtained from the Department for Environment, Food and Rural Affairs website (www.defra.gov. uk) or by telephoning 0800 316 6011.

Warm Deal (Scotland)

This scheme provides grants of up to £500 which can be put towards a number of energy-saving measures for certain households in Scotland. To be eligible for the scheme you or your spouse must own or rent your home, be over the age of 60 or be in receipt of state benefits. The grant will help to pay for cavity wall, loft, pipe or tank insulation, draught-proofing and energy-efficient lighting.

An assessor will visit your home to discuss your needs and

arrange for approved contractors to carry out the work. You will need to provide proof of your age if over 60, or proof that you are on state benefits, if under this age.

More information about the scheme can be obtained from the Scottish Executive website (www.scotland.gov.uk) or by telephoning 0800 072 0150.

Central Heating Programme (Scotland)

This scheme helps certain households in Scotland to improve the heating systems in their home. To qualify for the scheme people must:

- be resident in Scotland;

- own or rent their home, which must be their main or only residence;

- have been resident in the property for at least 12 months prior to the application, and intend to live in the property for at least 12 months after the work has been completed;

- live in a property that does not contain a central heating system, or in which the existing system is broken and beyond repair.

All successful applicants will be visited by an assessor who will recommend measures to improve the heating system. This could include a new central heating system, insulation, draught-proofing, smoke alarms and energy-saving light bulbs. More information about the scheme can be obtained from the Scottish Executive website (www.scotland.gov.uk) or by telephoning 0800 316 1653.

Warm Homes (Northern Ireland)

The Warm Homes scheme is funded by the Department for Social Development and managed by the Eaga Group. Through this scheme grants of up to £750 are provided for homeowners and tenants in Northern Ireland who are in receipt of certain benefits. More information about the scheme can be obtained from the Eaga website (www.eagagroup.com) or by telephoning 0800 181 667.

Low Carbon Buildings Programme

Through the Low Carbon Buildings Programme individual householders can apply for grants to help with the installation of renewable sources of energy for their homes. Larger grants are available for communities that decide to install renewable energy technology for community use. At the time of writing grants are offered at the levels given in Table A.1 for individual households. However, there have been some recent media reports about people being unsuccessful in their application – you should apply early and be aware that grants are subject to availability and strict criteria.

More information about these grants can be obtained from the DTI's Low Carbon Buildings Programme website (www.lowcarbon buildings.org.uk) or by telephoning 0800 915 0990.

Scottish Community and Householder Renewables Initiative

The Scottish Community and Householder Renewables Initiative offers grants and advice to people in Scotland who wish to develop renewable sources of energy. It is funded by the Scottish Executive and managed jointly by the EST and Highlands and Islands Enterprise. It is also possible for builders, developers and architects to apply for grants on behalf of future owners of houses they are building.

The initiative supports a range of renewable technologies that include the following:

- micro hydro-electric;
- micro wind;
- solar water heating;
- solar space heating;
- automated wood fuel heating systems (boilers and room heaters/ stoves);
- heat pumps (ground, air and water source);
- connections to the Lerwick District heating Network in Shetland (applies to heat exchanger only).

To qualify for a grant you must own the property where the renewable energy system is to be installed, obtain a quotation from an

Table A.1 Low Carbon Buildings Programme grants

Technology	Grant available
Solar photovoltaics	Maximum £3,000 per kWp installed, up to a maximum of £15,000 subject to an overall 50 per cent limit of the installed cost (exclusive of VAT)
Wind turbines	Maximum £1,000 per kW installed, up to a maximum of £5,000 subject to an overall 30 per cent limit of the installed cost (exclusive of VAT)
Small hydro	Maximum £1,000 per kW installed, up to a maximum of £5,000 subject to an overall 30 per cent limit of the installed cost (exclusive of VAT)
Solar thermal hot water	Maximum £400 regardless of size subject to an overall 30 per cent limit (exclusive of VAT)
Heat pumps	Maximum £1,200 regardless of size subject to a (ground/water/air source) overall 30 per cent limit (exclusive of VAT)
Bio-energy:	
1) Room heater/stoves with automated wood pellet feed	Maximum £600 regardless of size subject to an overall 20 per cent limit (exclusive of VAT)
2) Wood-fuelled boiler systems	Maximum of £1,500 regardless of size subject to an overall 30 per cent limit (exclusive of VAT)
Renewable CHP	Grant levels to be defined
Micro CHP	Grant levels to be defined
Fuel cells	Grant levels to be defined

accredited installer, and use an approved installer of an approved system. More information about the initiative can be obtained from the EST website (www.est.co.uk/schri) or by telephoning 0800 138 8858.

Enhanced capital allowances

The enhanced capital allowance (ECA) scheme was set up to encourage UK businesses to reduce carbon emissions which contribute to climate change. This scheme provides up-front tax relief, allowing businesses to claim 100 per cent first-year capital allowances against their taxable profits. ECAs bring forward this tax relief so that it can be set against the profits of a period earlier than would otherwise be the case. This means that you receive a reduction in your tax bill and a boost to your cashflow in the year in which the investment is made. If you are a property developer who pays corporation tax or income tax, you may be eligible for this scheme.

Only energy-saving products that meet the scheme's published energy-saving criteria can attract an ECA. The technologies that currently appear on the Energy Technology List and are therefore eligible for the ECA include:

- air-to-air energy recovery;
- automatic monitoring and targeting;
- boilers;
- combined heat and power;
- compact heat exchangers;
- compressed air equipment;
- heat pumps for space heating;
- HVAC zone controls;
- lighting;
- motors;
- pipework insulation;
- refrigeration equipment;
- solar thermal systems;
- terminal screens;
- variable speed drives;
- warm air and radiant heaters.

Most of these categories contain details of specific technologies that meet the funding criteria. Consult the ECA website for more information about the technologies you are intending to use (www. eca.gov.uk).

ECAs are claimed in the same way as other capital allowances on the corporation tax return for companies and the income tax return for individuals and partnerships. HM Revenue & Customs administers claims and will check for negligent or fraudulent claims. More information about making a claim can be obtained from the HMRC website (www.hmrc.gov.uk).

The energy efficiency commitment

In the United Kingdom the government requires energy companies to fund energy improvements in domestic homes. Under the energy efficiency commitment (EEC) companies are obliged to provide grants for homeowners to install cavity wall and loft insulation.

This scheme is aimed at homeowners but landlords can also take advantage of this scheme for some or all of their properties. At the time of writing the grant provides a £200 discount for cavity wall insulation and £150 for loft insulation. These grants change frequently, so for the most up-to-date information consult your local authority. The EST also has a network of advice centres located across England, Scotland, Wales and Northern Ireland. These centres are able to provide expert advice on the EEC, energy efficiency and information about grants and tax incentives for homeowners, landlords and developers who are hoping to make energy-efficient improvements to their properties. You can obtain contact details of your local energy efficiency advice centre by visiting www.est. org.uk/myhome/localadvice and entering your postcode in the box provided, or click on the relevant map location. Alternatively, you can use the form on the EST website to send an energy-related question to your local centre.

Stamp duty exemption

From April 2007 there will be no stamp duty payable on newly built zero-carbon homes for at least three years. At present it is unclear how the government will measure energy consumption. For example, will this definition relate to the building, the occupants or the construction techniques and materials? Some campaigners believe that there will be such stringent criteria attached to achieving exemption that it will be impossible for builders and developers to obtain. If you are hoping to build a zero-carbon home you will need to seek specialist advice at the planning and design stage.

DIY builders and converters refund scheme

If you are intending to build your own property, it is possible to claim a VAT refund on your main construction costs. However, you are excluded under this scheme if your development is for business purposes such as speculative development or to let to tenants. Rules and regulations are complex and you should seek further advice if you wish to take advantage of this scheme.

Useful organizations

Charitable groups and non-profit organizations

National Energy Foundation (NEF)

NEF is an educational charity registered in England that helps people in the United Kingdom by offering advice about safe and efficient energy use. The charity is controlled by an independent board of trustees whose concern is to protect the environment by avoiding the waste of energy. On its website you can find information about carbon dioxide emissions, energy ratings, saving energy, renewable and sustainable energy, and subscribe to the free newsletter.

National Energy Foundation
Davy Avenue
Knowlhill
Milton Keynes MK5 8NG
Tel: 01908 665555
Fax: 01908 665577
E-mail: info@nef.org.uk
Website: www.nef.org.uk

Centre for Alternative Technology (CAT)

CAT is a charity concerned with tackling issues that face our planet such as climate change, pollution and the waste of precious resources. CAT's visitor centre is situated in southern Snowdonia and is Europe's leading environmental display centre, covering a seven-acre site. At the centre you can see displays highlighting the power of wind, water and sun, and visit working examples of environmentally responsible buildings, energy conservation, organic growing and composting. CAT produces information leaflets on issues such as green tariffs, home heating with renewable energy, environmental building, investing in renewable energy, small-scale wind power, water harvesting and reusing grey water.

Centre for Alternative Technology
Machynlleth
Powys SY20 9AZ
Tel: 01654 705 950
Fax: 01654 702 782
Website: www.cat.org.uk

World Wildlife Fund

The World Wildlife Fund is the world's largest independent conservation charity, and was established in the United Kingdom in 1961. WWF-UK is involved in the 'One Million Sustainable Homes' project, which involves working with the government, industry and consumers to bring sustainable homes from the fringes of the housing sector to the mainstream. On its website you can download an information leaflet to find out more about this project. You can also access the 'housebuilder sustainability toolkit', which offers advice on sustainability issues to house-builders.

WWF-UK
Panda House, Weyside Park
Godalming
Surrey GU7 1XR
Tel: 01483 426444
Fax: 01483 426409
E-mail: england@wwf.org.uk
Website: www.wwf.org.uk

WWF Cymru
Baltic House, Mount Stuart Square
Cardiff CF10 5FH
Tel: 029 2045 4970
Fax: 029 2045 1306
E-mail: cymru@wwf.org.uk

WWF Northern Ireland
13 West Street

Carrickfergus
County Antrim BT38 7AR
Tel: 028 9335 5166
Fax: 028 9336 4448
E-mail: northernireland@wwf.org.uk

WWF Scotland
Little Dunkeld
Dunkeld
Perthshire PH8 0AD
Tel: 01350 728200
Fax: 01350 728201
E-mail: scotland@wwf.org.uk

Royal Horticultural Society (RHS)

The RHS is a UK charity dedicated to advancing horticulture and promoting good gardening. You can obtain information and advice about all aspects of horticulture, and the website contains a useful problem solver that helps you understand and solve problems that you may face in your garden, such as pests, plant disease and fungi.

Royal Horticultural Society
80 Vincent Square
London SW1P 2PE
Tel: 0845 260 5000
E-mail: info@rhs.org.uk
Website: www.rhs.org.uk

The Wildlife Trust

The Wildlife Trust is a partnership of 47 wildlife trusts across the United Kingdom. It is a UK charity dedicated to conserving wildlife habitats and species. You can find out more about its work, obtain useful publications and find information about your local trust on the website.

The Wildlife Trust
The Kiln, Waterside
Mather Road

Newark
Nottinghamshire NG24 1WT
Tel: 0870 036 7711
Fax: 0870 036 0101
E-mail: enquiry@wildlifetrusts.org
Website: www.wildlifetrusts.org

Garden Organic

Garden Organic is the working name of the Henry Doubleday
Research Association (HDRA), which is a charity for organic growing,
dedicated to helping gardeners, farmers and members of the public
who are interesting in organic methods. On its website you can find
useful information about all aspects of organic growing, including
composting, sourcing products, school projects and obtaining
organic food on a budget.

Garden Organic
Ryton Organic Gardens
Coventry
Warwickshire CV8 3LG
Tel: 024 7630 3517
Fax: 024 7663 9229
E-mail: enquiry@hydra.org.uk
Website: www.gardenorganic.org.uk

The Soil Association

The Soil Association is an environmental charity that promotes
sustainable, organic farming. Through Soil Association Certification
Ltd, organic certification is offered to farmers, growers, food
processors and packers, retailers, caterers, textile producers, health
and beauty manufacturers and importers, in the United Kingdom
and overseas. You can look for this certification when checking to see
that the products you are buying are organic. The Soil Association
website contains useful information on living an organic lifestyle.

The Soil Association
Bristol House, 40–56 Victoria Street
Bristol BS1 6BY

Tel: 0117 314 5000
Fax: 0117 314 5001
E-mail: info@soilassociation.org
Website: www.soilassociation.org

Pesticide Action Network UK (PAN UK)

PAN UK is an independent, non-profit organization that promotes
healthy food, agriculture and an environment that will provide
food and meet public health needs without dependence on toxic
chemicals, and without harm to food producers and agricultural
workers. On its website you can find information and publications on
a wide variety of issues concerning the avoidance of toxic chemicals,
controlling pests in the garden and home, and disposing safely of
unwanted pesticides.

Pesticide Action Network UK
Development House, 56–64 Leonard Street
London EC2A 4JH
Tel: 020 7065 0905
Fax: 020 7064 0907
E-mail: admin@pan-uk.org
Website: www.pan-uk.org

Advisory groups

Energy Saving Trust (EST)

The EST was established as part of the government's action plan in
response to the 1992 Earth Summit in Rio de Janeiro which addressed
worldwide concerns on sustainable development issues. The EST
works in partnership with other organizations and communities to
encourage energy efficiency and the use of renewable energy sources
such as wind and solar power. Its work includes the promotion
of cleaner fuels for transport, and better insulation and heating
efficiency for homes and other buildings.

The EST develops and manages programmes on behalf of the
UK government, which include awareness-raising among local
communities, the general public and commercial organizations;
the production and distribution of a wide range of information

documents and publications; and grants for innovative technologies and techniques.

Energy Saving Trust (England)
21 Dartmouth Street
London SW1H 9BP
Tel: 020 7222 0101
Fax: 020 7654 2460
Website: www.est.org.uk

Energy Saving Trust (Scotland)
112/2 Commercial Street
Leith
Edinburgh EH6 6NF
Tel: 0131 555 7900
Fax: 0131 555 7919

Energy Saving Trust (Wales)
Wales Albion House, Oxford Street
Nantgarw
Cardiff CF15 7TR
Tel: 01443 845030
Fax: 01433 845940

Energy Saving Trust (Northern Ireland)
Enterprise House, 55/59 Adelaide Street
Belfast BT2 8FE
Tel: 028 9072 6006
Fax: 028 9023 9907

Local energy efficiency advice centres

The EST has a network of advice centres located across England, Scotland, Wales and Northern Ireland. These centres are able to provide expert advice on energy efficiency, and information about grants and tax incentives for landlords hoping to make energy-efficient improvements to their properties. You can obtain contact details of your local centre by visiting www.est.org.uk/myhome/localadvice and entering your postcode in the box provided. Alternatively, you can use the form on the EST website to send an energy-related question to your local centre.

Community Action for Energy

This organization is a network of people who share a common interest in community energy projects and ideas. It is a programme from the EST that is designed to 'promote and facilitate local community-based energy projects'. Membership is free and once you become a member you can receive information about training sessions, new initiatives, local funding opportunities and relevant local news.

On its website you can access a database of funding opportunities. This enables you to search by keyword, fund name, type of funding, eligible regions and funding organizations. This is a very useful database for finding information about grants and schemes that may benefit you as a homeowner, landlord, developer or tenant. More information about the Community Action for Energy network can be obtained from www.est.org.uk/cafe or by telephoning 08701 261 444.

Home improvement agencies

Home improvements agencies (HIAs) are small, non-profit-making bodies that are funded by local authorities through the Supporting People Programme. They are managed locally by housing associations, local authorities or charitable organizations. The main functions of HIAs are to support vulnerable people in their quest to remain independent in their homes; help people access funds and resources to make home improvements; and provide information on home insurance, loans and equity release. If you are a vulnerable homeowner or a landlord letting your property to tenants who are older, disabled or on low incomes, you can seek advice from your local HIA.

More information about HIAs can be obtained from your local authority or by contacting Foundations, which is the national coordinating body for home improvement agencies in England. On its website you can find contact details of your nearest HIA.

Foundations
Bleaklow House, Howard Town Mill
Glossop
Derbyshire SK13 8HT
Tel: 01457 891 909
Fax: 01457 869 361

E-mail: foundations@cel.co.uk
Website: www.cel.co.uk/foundations

The Pensions Advisory Service (TPAS)

TPAS is an independent, voluntary organization that is grant-aided by the Department for Work and Pensions. TPAS offers useful and down-to-earth information about pensions, helping to explain complex rules and regulations in a way that can be understood by the layperson. It will also help members of the public who have a problem, complaint or dispute with their occupational or private pension arrangements.

The Pensions Advisory Service
11 Belgrave Road
London SW1V 1RB
Tel: 0845 6012 823
Fax: 020 7233 8016
E-mail: enquiries@pensionsadvisoryservice.org.uk
Website: www.pensionsadvisoryservice.org.uk

Commercial organizations

Eaga Group

The Eaga Group delivers energy-efficient programmes on behalf of central government, the devolved national governments, major utility companies and private customers. You can apply for energy efficiency grants through this company. Online applications for grants can be made via the website. This includes the following schemes:

■ Home Energy Efficiency Scheme (Wales);

■ Warm Front (England);

■ Warm Deal (Scotland);

■ Central Heating Programme (Scotland);

■ Warm Homes Scheme (Northern Ireland).

Contact the Eaga Group or visit its website for more information:

Eaga House, Archbold Terrace
Newcastle upon Tyne NE2 1DB
Tel: 0191 247 3800
Fax: 0191 247 3802
E-mail: enquiries@eaga.co.uk
Website: www.eagagroup.com

The Carbon Trust

The Carbon Trust is an independent company funded by the government. The role of the company is to help the UK 'move to a low carbon economy by helping business and the public sector reduce carbon emission now and capture the commercial opportunities of low carbon technologies'. The company produces useful information on climate change and energy efficiency for businesses, provides energy efficiency loans of £5,000–200,000, and advises on enhanced capital allowances for business (see Chapter 9).

The Carbon Trust
8th floor, 3 Clement's Inn
London WC2A 2AZ
Tel: 0800 085 2005
Fax: 020 7170 7020
E-mail: customercentre@carbontrust.co.uk
Website: www.carbontrust.co.uk

The Carbon Trust in Wales
Albion House, Oxford Street
Nantgarw
Cardiff CF15 7TR
Tel: 01443 845944
E-mail: contactwales@thecarbontrust.co.uk

The Carbon Trust in Scotland
Brunel Building, James Watt Avenue
Scottish Enterprise Technology Park
East Kilbride G75 0QD
Tel: 01355 581810
E-mail: john.stocks@thecarbontrust.co.uk

The Carbon Trust in Northern Ireland
Unit 9, Northern Ireland Science Park
The Innovation Centre
Queen's Road, Queen's Island
Belfast BT3 9DT
Tel: 02890 737912
E-mail: geoff.smyth@thecarbontrust co.uk

Ethical Investors Group

The Ethical Investors Group has been established to provide a specialist financial advice service to people who care about the world and its preservation. Advice is offered to individuals, charities, not-for-profit groups and commercial organizations. Although this is a commercial organization, 50 per cent of the profit earned from commission and fees is distributed to charities and groups nominated by its clients. Contact the group for information about its fees.

On its website you can use the Ethical Fund Directory, which is a comprehensive list of all ethical funds available in the United Kingdom. Each entry in the directory includes a special 'ethical rating' code, rating funds on three criteria: humanist, animal welfare and environmental performance. Information is also provided on ethical ISAs, mortgages, life assurance and pensions.

Ethical Investors Group
Montpellier House, 47 Rodney Road
Cheltenham GL50 1HX
Tel: 01242 539 848
Fax: 01242 539 851
E-mail: info@ethicalinvestors.co.uk
Website: www.ethicalinvestors.co.uk

Ethical Investment Research Services

The Ethical Investment Research Service provides independent research into the social, environmental and ethical performance of companies from Europe, North America and Asia Pacific. It provides a wide range of information to individuals and organizations, but does not offer independent advice or recommend particular funds. On its website you can obtain information about all types of SRI.

Ethical Investment Research Services
80–84 Bondway
London SW8 1SF
Tel: 020 7840 5700
Fax: 020 7735 5323
E-mail: ethics@eiris.org
Website: www.eiris.org

British Fenestration Rating Council (BFRC)

The BFRC has developed and operates a UK national rating system
for the thermal performance of fenestration products. On the website
you can search for the best-performing windows in terms of energy
efficiency, and search for an installer, manufacturer and supplier of
energy-saving windows.

British Fenestration Rating Council Ltd
44–48 Borough High Street
London SE1 1XB
Tel: 020 7403 9200
Fax: 0870 042 4266
E-mail: info@bfrc.org
Website: www.brfc.org

Building Research Establishment Ltd (BRE)

BRE is a collection of research scientists, engineers, architects, surveyors, psychologists, administrators, managers and others who
bring together their knowledge and expertise to advise on sustainable
construction and the built environment. They provide a variety of
consultancy, testing and commissioned research services. The BRE
bookshop provides a full range of sustainable construction books.

Building Research Establishment Ltd
Bucknalls Lane
Watford WD25 9XX
Tel: 01923 664 000
E-mail: enquiries@bre.co.uk
Website: www.bre.co.uk

Government departments

Department for Communities and Local Government

You can obtain information about the new home information pack, along with other useful housing information, from the Department for Communities and Local Government (DCLG).

Department for Communities and Local Government
Eland House, Bressenden Place
London SW1E 5DU
Tel: 020 7944 4400
Fax: 020 7944 9645
E-mail: contactus@communities.gsi.gov.uk
Website: www.communities.gov.uk

Sustainable Energy Policy Division

For more information about government policy issues relating to energy efficiency, consult the Sustainable Energy Policy Division of DEFRA.

Sustainable Energy Policy Division
DEFRA
6/H15, Ashdown House, 123 Victoria Street
London SW1E 6DE
Tel: 020 7082 8709
Fax: 020 7082 8708

Companies House

The main functions of Companies House are to incorporate and dissolve limited companies, examine and store company information delivered under the Companies Act and make this information available to the public.

Companies House
Crown Way, Maindy
Cardiff CF14 3UT
Tel: 0870 33 33 363
E-mail: enquiries@companies-house.gov.uk
Website: www.companieshouse.gov.uk

Planning Inspectorate

The Planning Inspectorate processes planning and enforcement appeals and holds inquiries into local development plans in England and Wales.

Planning Inspectorate
Temple Quay House, 2 The Square
Bristol BS1 6PN
Tel: 0117 372 6372
Fax: 0117 372 8443
E-mail: enquiries@planning-pins.gsi.gov.uk
Website: www.planning-inspectorate.gov.uk

Office of Fair Trading (OFT)

The OFT provides useful advice for anyone who needs to draw up a contract or sign a contract drawn up by another person.

Office of Fair Trading
Fleetbank House, 2–6 Salisbury Square
London EC4Y 8JX
Tel: 08457 22 44 99
E-mail: enquiries@oft.gsi.gov.uk
Website: www.oft.gov.uk

Trade organizations and membership groups

National Association of Estate Agents (NAEA)

NAEA is the largest professional estate agency organization in the United Kingdom. It represents almost 10,000 members and is committed to raising professional standards for those working within the property market. All members must operate to a professional code of practice and rules of conduct. A list of members is available on the website.

National Association of Estate Agents
Arbon House, 21 Jury Street
Warwick CV34 4EH
Tel: 01926 496 800
Fax: 01926 400 953
E-mail: info@naea.co.uk
Website: www.naea.co.uk

The Ombudsman for Estate Agents (OEA)

The OEA has been established to provide a free, fair and independent service to buyers and sellers of residential property in the United Kingdom. You can find contact details of members in your area from the website, access housing survey information and find out about the code of practice.

Ombudsman for Estate Agents
Beckett House, 4 Bridge Street
Salisbury
Wilts SP1 2LX
Tel: 01722 333 306
Fax: 01722 332 296
E-mail: admin@oea.co.uk
Website: www.oea.co.uk

National Association of Loft Insulation Contractors (NALIC)

NALIC represents the loft insulation contracting industry and its suppliers. You can obtain information about loft insulation and a list of members in your area from NALIC.

National Association of Loft Insulation Contractors
PO Box 12
Haslemere
Surrey GU27 3AH

Tel: 01428 654 011
Fax: 01428 651 401

British Wind Energy Association (BWEA)

BWEA is the trade and professional body for the wind and marine renewables industries. The primary aim of the association is to promote the use of wind power around the United Kingdom, both inshore and offshore. If you are interested in installing your own wind turbine you can obtain an information pack and a list of small wind turbine suppliers from the BWEA.

British Wind Energy Association
Renewable Energy House
1 Aztec Row, Berners Road
London N1 0PW
Tel: 020 7689 1960
Fax: 020 7689 1969
E-mail: info@bwea.com
Website: www.bwea.com

Association of Home Information Pack Providers (AHIPP)

AHIPP was founded in June 2005 to represent people and organizations involved in the production and preparation of home information packs. On its website you can obtain information about what the organization does, along with links to organizations providing home information pack services.

Association of Home Information Pack Providers
3 Savile Row
London W1S 3PB
Tel: 0870 950 7739
Fax: 01858 454 714
E-mail: info@hipassociation.co.uk
Website: www.hipassociation.co.uk

Straw Bale Building Association (SBBA)

SBBA is an informal association of people who have an interest in straw bale building. Members include environmental enthusiasts, sustainable builders, architects and building officials. The SBBA offers courses, workshops, books and videos for anyone interested in straw bale construction.

Straw Bale Building Association
Hollinroyd Farm, Butts Lane
Todmorden OL14 8RJ
Tel: 01442 825 421
E-mail: info@stawbalebuildingassociation.org.uk
Website: www.srawbalebuildingassociation.org.uk

UK Social Investment Forum (UKSIF)

UKSIF was launched in 1991 and is a membership network for UK socially responsible investment (SRI). Its primary purpose is to promote and encourage the development of SRI among UK investors. Members include retail and institutional fund managers, financial advisers, SRI research providers, consultants, trade unions, banks, building societies, NGOs and interested individuals. A member directory is available on the website, along with useful information about SRI.

UK Social Investment Forum
Holywell Centre, 1 Phipp Street
London EC2A 4PS
Tel: 020 7749 9950
E-mail: info@uksif.org
Website: www.uksif.org

Ethical Trading Initiative (ETI)

The ETI is an alliance of companies, NGOs and trade union organizations. It exists to ensure that the working conditions of workers producing for the UK market meet or exceed international labour standards. On the website you can find more information about ethical trade.

Ethical Trading Initiative
2nd floor, Cromwell House
14 Fulwood Place
London WC1V 6HZ
Tel: 020 7404 1463
Fax: 020 7831 7852
E-mail: eti@eti.org.uk
Website: www.ethicaltrade.org.uk

Royal Institute of British Architects (RIBA)

RIBA is a member organization with over 30,000 members worldwide.
You can find an architect using one of its online directories.

Royal Institute of British Architects
RIBA Client Services
66 Portland Place
London W1N 4AD
Tel: 020 7580 5533
Fax: 020 7255 1541
E-mail: info@inst.riba.org
Website: www.riba.org

Royal Institute of Chartered Surveyors (RICS)

RICS is the largest organization for professionals working in property,
land and construction worldwide. RICS members have to adhere to
a strict code of conduct and are required to update their skills and
knowledge continually. All members must have proper insurance,
and customers are protected by a RICS formal complaints service.

Royal Institute of Chartered Surveyors
RICS Contact Centre
Surveyor Court, Westwood Way
Coventry CV4 8JE
Tel: 0870 333 1600
Fax: 020 7334 3811
E-mail: contactrics@rics.org
Website: www.rics.org

Council of Licensed Conveyancers

The Council of Licensed Conveyancers is the regulatory body for licensed conveyancers, who are qualified specialist property lawyers. You can obtain the contact details of a conveyancer in your area by using the online directory.

Council of Licensed Conveyancers
16 Glebe Road
Chelmsford
Essex CM1 1QG
Tel: 01245 349599
Fax: 01245 341300
Website: www.theclc.gov.uk

Association of Independent Inventory Clerks (AIIC)

AIIC was set up in 1996 to represent inventory clerks and provide information to tenants and landlords. Members must agree to abide by a code of practice. On the website you can find information about the tenancy deposit scheme and details about what is meant by fair wear and tear.

Association of Independent Inventory Clerks
Central Office, Willow House
16 Commonfields
West End
Surrey GU24 9HZ
Tel/Fax: 01276 855388
E-mail: centraloffice@aiic.uk.com
Website: www.aiic.uk.com

Association for Environment Conscious Building (AECB)

AECB is a network of individuals and companies with a common aim of promoting sustainable building.

Association for Environment Conscious Building
PO Box 32
Llandysull SA44 5ZA

Tel: 0845 456 9773
E-mail: graigoffice@aecb.net
Website: www.aecb.net

Renewable Energy Association

The Renewable Energy Association is the trade body for renewable energy producers in the United Kingdom. Although it is unable to provide answers to specific queries from members of the public, its website contains useful and detailed information about all types of renewable energy, and you can search their database for a member in your area.

Renewable Energy Association
17 Waterloo Place
London SW1Y 4AR
Tel: 020 7747 1830
Fax: 020 7925 2715
E-mail: use enquiry form on website
Website: www.r-e-a.net

Guarantee agencies and licensing groups

Cavity Insulation Guarantee Agency (CIGA)

CIGA is an independent agency that provides independent 25-year guarantees for cavity wall insulation fitted by registered installers. The guarantee covers materials and workmanship, and is available to subsequent owners of the property. CIGA will investigate complaints and, where necessary, ensure that remedial work is carried out free of charge.

Cavity Insulation Guarantee Agency
CIGA House, 3 Vimy Court
Vimy Road
Leighton Buzzard
Bedfordshire LU7 1FG
Tel: 01525 853 300
Fax: 01525 385 926
E-mail: info@ciga.co.uk
Website: www.ciga.co.uk

The Fairtrade Foundation

The Fairtrade Foundation licenses the FAIRTRADE mark to products in the United Kingdom that meet international Fairtrade standards. This mark is an independent consumer label that appears on products as a guarantee that disadvantaged producers in the developing world are getting a better deal. You can find out more about Fairtrade products and suppliers on its website.

The Fairtrade Foundation
Room 204, 16 Baldwin's Gardens
London EC1N 7RJ
Tel: 020 7405 5942
Fax: 020 7405 5943
E-mail: mail@fairtrade.org.uk
Website: www.fairtrade.org.uk

Useful websites

Charitable groups

www.nef.org.uk
This is the website of the National Energy Foundation. On the website you can obtain useful information about sustainable and renewable energies and the Energy Efficiency Accreditation Scheme, advice for children and schools and take part in a renewable energy quiz and survey.

www.wildaboutgardens.org
This is a new project from the RHS and wildlife trusts that aims to bring together the worlds of gardening and nature conservation for the benefit of people and wildlife. On the website you can find useful information and advice about establishing a wildlife garden.

Advisory groups

www.est.org.uk
This is the website of the Energy Saving Trust. On the website you can find useful information about insulation, double glazing, home efficiency checks, building regulations, grants and loans, a database of approved contractors, renewable energy sources, low-carbon buildings and much more.

www.centralheating.co.uk
This is the website of the Heating and Hot Water Industry Council (HHIC). It is an independent organization which aims to provide unbiased information on all heating and hot water matters. On its website you can find information about saving energy and grants, find a registered installer and order a heat loss calculator. This is an

accurate and simple programme that helps you to calculate how much heat is being lost in your home.

Commercial organizations

www.carbontrust.co.uk
This is the website of the Carbon Trust. On the website you can obtain information about climate change, saving energy, managing carbon, loans, tax relief, new technology research and development, business development and free energy surveys.

www.ethicalinvestment.org.uk
This is the website of the Ethical Investors Association (EIA), which is an association of financial advisers from around the United Kingdom who promote ethical and socially responsible investment. The aim of the organization is to increase public access to financial advice on ethical and socially responsible investment, and raise standards among financial advisers offering this type of advice. On the website you can obtain useful advice about ethical investment and access a database of ethical financial advisers in the United Kingdom.

www.brebookshop.com
This in an online bookstore selling books, videos and software on all topics related to the built environment sector. You can search the bookstore by title, author, ISBN, keyword and publisher. You can obtain specialist books from this site that might be difficult to obtain elsewhere.

www.greenbuildingstore.co.uk
This is the website of the Green Building Store, which is owned and run by Environmental Construction Products Ltd. This company has specialized in environmentally sensitive building products since 1995, and is committed to energy-efficient, sustainable and healthy buildings. On the website you can search the full product range for glazing, guttering, insulation, paints and wood finishes, sanitary ware, taps and water saving products, timber preservation, water-efficient WCs, and windows and doors.

www.salvoweb.com
Salvo is a partnership that aims to support dealers that hold stocks of architectural salvage, reclaimed building materials, demolition

salvage and recycled materials. Where possible it encourages fair trade and eco-friendly activities. Contact details for dealers, suppliers and craftspeople can be obtained from the website.

www.greenelectricity.org
This is the website of the Green Electricity Marketplace. You can select a region in which you live or to which you want to move and find out about the local suppliers that offer green tariffs. Prices and services are compared, along with useful information about choosing a suitable supplier and advice about the different types of renewable energy sources.

www.greenmoves.com
GreenMoves is an advertising website that helps to sell environmentally friendly homes in the United Kingdom and overseas. It is a limited liability company that reinvests its profits back into the development of the website to offer a better service to its customers. In the future it hopes to be able to use some of its profits to offer small grants to help promote the cause of eco-friendly homes.

www.ernest-charles.com
This is the website of Earnest Charles, a company that specializes in products for garden wildlife, including safe and humane deterrents for pests, soil improvers, bird seed, feeders and baths, books and gifts. The company helps to develop bird feed products and contributes to wildlife trusts. More information and its online store can be accessed from the website.

www.naturalgardening.co.uk
On this website you will find a range of fertilizers and compost balancers that will help you to enrich your garden soil in an organic way.

www.impactpublishing.co.uk
Impact Publishing specializes in modern, practical guides to gardening, lifestyle choices and the environment. On its website you can find books about creating wildlife gardens and ponds, green parenting, growing fruit and vegetables, and producing perfect lawns.

www.greenpestco.com
The Green Pest Company is a family-run business that supplies environmentally friendly products to control pests.

www.recycleworks.co.uk
This company manufactures and sells recycling products such as composting equipment, water butts, waste organizations systems and shredders. It also has a 'giveaway' service that enables users to offer unwanted items in good condition free of charge.

www.wigglywigglers.co.uk
This company offers sustainable products ranging from various type of worm composting equipment to bird boxes and feeders. On the website you can find useful advice about worm composting.

www.livingclean.co.uk
On this website you can obtain environmentally friendly cleaning products which are based on natural products and free from harmful chemicals. The company also offers a cleaning service for landlords, using its environmentally friendly products to clean carpets, upholstery, ovens and bathrooms.

Government departments, schemes and programmes

www.communities.gov.uk
This is the Department for Communities and Local Government website. Here you can find comprehensive information about the Housing Act 2004, including information about the new Housing Health and Safety Rating System (HHSRS) assessment.

www.eca.gov.uk
On this website you can obtain details about the enhanced capital allowance (ECA) scheme, and information about the technologies that are included within this scheme.

www.hmrc.gov.uk
On this website you can obtain more information about claiming ECAs, along with information about all other tax issues.

www.lowcarbonbuildings.org.uk
This is the website of the Low Carbon Buildings Programme. On this site you can find information about grants available for the installation of renewable energy technologies.

www.fsa.gov.uk
The Financial Services Authority (FSA) is the independent regulator set up by the government to look after the financial services industry and protect customers. On its website you can obtain information on financial planning, insurance, pensions, mortgages, and warnings about scams, people and companies to avoid.

www.neighbourhood.statistics.gov.uk
You can find statistics for local areas on a wide range of subjects, which include population, crime, health and housing, on this site. By entering the postcode of the property in which you are interested you can obtain summary statistics of the area based on the 2001 Census. A useful table shows you the average house prices of different types of property in your area, your county and in England and Wales. You can also view the statistics by subject: 'housing' reveals many different tables, ranging from accommodation type to occupancy rating.

www.landregisteronline.gov.uk
Land Register Online provides easy access to details of more than 20 million registered properties in England and Wales. You can download copies of title plans and registers in PDF format for £3 each, payable online by credit card.

www.ros.gov.uk
This is the website of the Registers of Scotland Executive Agency. It provides information about Scotland's land and property. On the website, for a small fee, you can find out about property prices anywhere in Scotland.

Trade organizations and professional associations

www.aecb.net
The Association for Environment Conscious Building (AECB) is a network of individuals and companies with a common aim of promoting sustainable building. On the website you can find information about improving the environmental performance of your property; choosing eco-friendly products and avoiding damaging chemicals; using timber; and planning and developing eco-friendly properties.

www.british-hydro.org
The British Hydropower Association represents the interests of people who are involved in the production of hydro power in the United Kingdom, from large companies to individuals and charities. On its website you can find comprehensive information about producing hydro power and the costs involved.

www.nationalinsulationassociation.org.uk
The National Insulation Association (NIA) represents the manufacturers and installers of all types of insulation and draught-proofing. On this website you can find details of an installer and manufacturer in your area by accessing the Register of Members and the Register of Manufacturers. The website contains useful information about insulation and draught-proofing techniques and materials.

www.ukrha.org
The UK Rainwater Harvesting Association (UK-RHA) is a limited company by guarantee that serves to act as a focal point for organizations with business interests in the rainwater harvesting industry. On its website you can access more information about rainwater harvesting and obtain contact details of members.

www.thepfs.org
The Personal Finance Society (PFS) is the merged professional association of the Life Insurance Association and the Society of Financial Advisers. Visit this website to use the online directory of financial advisers in the United Kingdom. The website contains useful information about various types of investment and obtaining financial advice.

Directories

www.unbiased.co.uk
This is the Independent Financial Adviser Promotion (IFAP) website. It is a directory of 9,000 individuals and organizations, covering over 90 per cent of registered IFAs in the United Kingdom. On the website you can search for an IFA in your area by gender, investment type, qualification and the method in which you would like to pay for advice.

Campaign groups and NGOs

www.climnet.org
The Climate Action Network (CAN) is a worldwide network of over 365 NGOs working to promote action on limiting the human influence on climate change. On its website you can find information about climate change trends and signals, along with information about CAN offices.

www.climate-concern.com
Climate Concern UK is a campaign group focused on increasing public understanding of the dangers of climate change. On the website you can obtain information about the effects of climate change, and useful information to combat scepticism over climate change.

Further reading

Callard, S and Millia, D (2001) *The Complete Book of Green Living*, Carlton, London

Chiras, D (2002) *The Solar House: Passive heating and cooling*, Chelsea Green, Post Mills, Vermont

Chiras, D (2004) *The New Ecological Home: A complete guide to green building options*, Chelsea Green, Post Mills, Vermont

Clift, J and Cuthbert, A (2006) *Energy: Use less, save more*, Green Books, Totnes

Clift, J and Cuthbert, A *(2006) Water: Use less, save more*, Green Books, Totnes

Dawson, C (2006) *The Complete Guide to Property Development for the Small Investor*, Kogan Page, London

Dean, A (2003) *Green by Design*, Gibbs M Smith, Layton, Utah

Hall, K (ed) (2005) *The Green Building Bible*, Green Building Press, Llandysul

Hancock, J (2005) *An Investor's Guide to Ethical and Socially Responsible Investment Funds: A unique analysis of UK based investment funds*, Kogan Page, London

Harland, E (1999) *Eco-Renovation: Ecological home improvement guide*, Resurgence Books, London

Harris, C and Borer, P (2005) *The Whole House Book: Ecological building design and materials*, 2nd edn, Centre for Alternative Technology, Machynlleth

Hegarty, M (2000) *The Little Book of Living Green*, Nightingale Press, Royston

Kennedy, J F, Smith, M G and Wanek, C (2002) *The Art of Natural Building: Design, construction, resources*, New Society, Gabriola Island, British Colombia

Hymers, P (2006) *Converting to an Eco-Friendly Home: The complete handbook*, New Holland, London

Jones, E (2006) *Go Make a Difference*, 3rd edn, Think Books, London

Litchfield, C (ed) (2005) *The Organic Directory 2006*, Green Books, Totnes

Norris, S (2005) *Superkids! 250 incredible ways for kids to save the planet*, Think Books, London

Plowright, T. (2007) *Eco-centres and Courses*, Green Books, Totnes

Roberts, J (2003) *Good Green Homes*, Gibbs M Smith, Layton, Utah

Roaf, S (2001) *Eco House: A design guide*, Architectural Press, Oxford

Roulac, J (1998) *Backyard Composting*, Green Books, Totnes

Scott, N (2003) *Composting for All*, Green Books, Totnes

Scott, N (2004) *Reduce, Reuse, Recycle! An easy household guide*, Green Books, Totnes

Siegle, L (2001) *Green Living in the Urban Jungle*, Green Books, Totnes

Smith, P (2003) *Eco-Refurbishment: A practical guide to creating an energy efficient home*, Architectural Press, Oxford

Snell, C and Callahan, T (2005) *Building Green: A complete how-to guide to alternative building methods*, Lark Books, Asheville, North Carolina

Trask, C (2006) *It's Easy Being Green: A handbook for earth friendly living*, Gibbs Smith, Layton, Utah

Warren, P (2003) *How to Store your Garden Produce: The key to self sufficiency*, Green Books, Totnes

Index

Index of advertsiers